18359   294.6

D0230734

The **Sikh** Experience

Philip Emmett

seeking religion

Hodder & Stoughton

A MEMBER OF THE HODDER HEADLINE GROUP

Acknowledgements

To Rajinder Singh Basson, Nirmal Kaur Basson and their daughters Amarjot Kaur and Simran Kaur.

The author would like to thank Harjinder Boparai at HSB Productions Ltd for permission to reproduce the quote on page 59.

Words in heavy text **like this** are explained in the glossary on page 63.

The publisher would like to thank the following for permission to reproduce copyright photographs in this book:

J Allan Cash Photolibrary: p43t; Hulton Getty Picture Collection Ltd: p51; David Rose: p27; Malkit Singh: p59.

All remaining photographs courtesy of Philip Emmett.

Every effort has been made to contact the holders of copyright material but if any have been inadvertently overlooked, the publisher will be pleased to make the necessary alterations at the first opportunity.

CE = Common Era
BCE = Before the Common Era

CE corresponds to AD, and BCE corresponds to BC. The years are the same, but CE and BCE can be used by anyone, regardless of their religion.

18359

AYLESBURY COLLEGE

LIBRARY

Orders: please contact Bookpoint Ltd, 39 Milton Park, Abingdon, Oxon OX14 4TD. Telephone: (44) 01235 400414, Fax: (44) 01235 400454. Lines are open from 9.00–6.00, Monday to Saturday, with a 24 hour message answering service. Email address: orders@bookpoint.co.uk

British Library Cataloguing in Publication Data
A catalogue record for this title is available from The British Library

ISBN 0 340 74772 2

First published 1992
Second edition 2000
Impression number   10 9 8 7 6 5 4 3 2 1
Year   2005 2004 2003 2002 2001 2000

Copyright © 1992, 2000 Philip Emmett

All rights reserved. No part of this publication may be reproduced or transmitted in any form or by any means, electronic or mechanical, including photocopy, recording, or any information storage and retrieval system, without permission in writing from the publisher or under licence from the Copyright Licensing Agency Limited. Further details of such licences (for reprographic reproduction) may be obtained from the Copyright Licensing Agency Limited, of 90 Tottenham Court Road, London W1P 9HE.

Cover photo from Corbis
All illustrations supplied by Daedalus with special thanks to John McIntyre.
Typeset by Wearset, Boldon, Tyne and Wear.
Printed for Hodder & Stoughton Educational, a division of Hodder Headline Plc, 338 Euston Road, London NW1 3BH by Printer Trento, Italy.

Contents

Guru Nanak

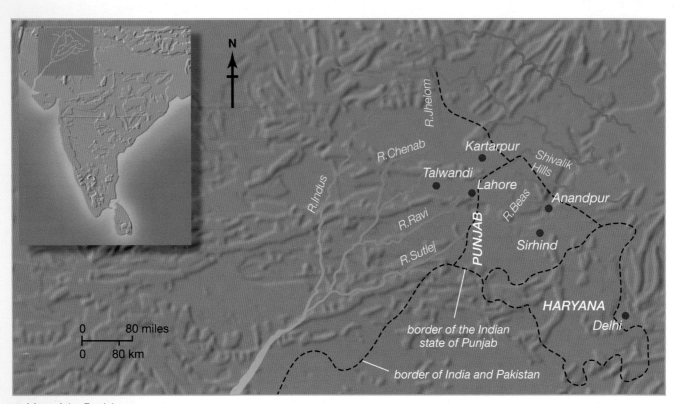

▲ *Map of the Punjab*

The land of the five rivers in northern India has always been known as the Punjab. The word 'panj' means five. The Punjab is a very fertile area where much food is grown. It also has other important resources for hot countries, such as salt.

As a result of this, ancient rulers wanted to own the Punjab – and invaders from the north would conquer the Punjab on their way to central India. It also lies on the ancient land trade routes that passed from Europe and the Middle East to central India, China and other far eastern countries.

As the traders passed through and the invaders came, the people of the Punjab heard of different beliefs and ways of worshipping God. They were especially influenced by the Hindu beliefs of India and the Muslim religion. This was the religion of the rulers of parts of northern India during the fourteenth to the seventeenth centuries CE.

Guru Nanak was born at Talwandi near Lahore in the Punjab in 1469 CE. He was the first of ten **Gurus** (religious teachers) who founded the Sikh religion. His birthplace is now known as Nankana Sahib and is part of Pakistan. His birthday is celebrated each year in early November, the actual date being set by the full moon.

● It is through actions that some come nearer to God and some wander away.

Guru Nanak

▲ *Guru Nanak*

However, work did not really interest him and he spent much time on his own, praying, seeking the truth and helping others.

> ● Lord, Thy grace and mercy fall on the land. Where the lowly are cherished.
>
> *Guru Nanak*

In a **spiritual** experience he entered a river and was taken into the presence of God. He returned three days later with the **mission** to teach men and women to pray, do works of charity and live in a pure way.

Guru Nanak was the son of a high **caste** Hindu. Stories of his childhood and youth were collected in the **Janam Sakhis**. These stories showed that he was going to be a great religious teacher. He amazed both Hindu priests and learned Muslims by his wisdom and intelligence. Some stories show his concern for the poor and needy. On one occasion he spent the money given to him by his father helping the poor instead of using it for trade.

Other stories about his childhood include amazing and unexplained events which show his religious importance. Once, a normally deadly cobra shaded his face from the heat of the sun. On another occasion he allowed the cattle he was tending to wander into and eat the grass from a nearby field. The owner of the field was very angry but the field was later found to be completely undamaged. Guru Nanak himself always denied that he possessed any power to work miracles, except the name of God.

It's a sign! He's going to be a great teacher.

▲ *Scenes from the early life of Guru Nanak*

> ● Mighty is the Lord, and great His gifts.
>
> *Guru Nanak*

In those days people married young. Guru Nanak was probably only sixteen years old when he married. He and his wife had two sons. His sister and brother-in-law found him a job as an accountant for a Muslim member of the ruling family. He worked there until he was about thirty years old. He was well known for his honesty.

1 Write a sentence to explain the terms 'Guru' and 'Janam Sakhi'.

2 Look at the map of the Punjab on page 4. Find a map of modern Pakistan and India and find out where the places named in this story are.

3 **a)** How do you think the stories of Guru Nanak as a young man show that he was going to have an important religious future?

   b) What explanations can you think of for the miracles that took place?

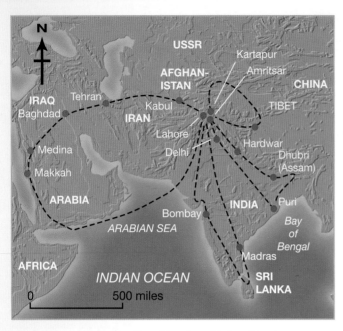

▲ *The places visited by Guru Nanak on his teaching journeys*

After Guru Nanak's experience in the river he went on four great teaching journeys. The map opposite shows where he went on these journeys. He visited the holy places in the north-east, south and west of India, Sri Lanka and Tibet. He went to the Muslim holy places of Makkah, Madina and those in Iraq and Iran. His friend Mardana, a talented Muslim musician, always went with him on his journeys. He did this because at that time people could not read and write. Learning a song helped people to remember what he had taught.

> ● There is neither Hindu nor Muslim so whose path shall I follow? I shall follow God's path. God is neither Hindu nor Muslim and the path which I follow is God's.
>
> *Guru Nanak*

He taught that all people are equal before God. This was a challenging message in a land where people were divided by caste.

▼ *Some of the things Guru Nanak did on his teaching journeys*

In 1521 CE Guru Nanak established a new town called Kartarpur, 'the seat of God', where his **disciples**, or **Sikhs**, could hear his teachings. It was a community where Nanak and his Sikhs could work, learn and pray together. When he finally returned from his travels he started a free kitchen or **langar**. Here, free meals were served to visitors. People ate together; it did not matter who they were.

Guru Nanak died on 22 September 1539 CE. He appointed Lehna, one of his disciples, to be his successor as Guru. You can read about him in the next chapter.

▲ How Lehna was chosen to be the next Guru

1 Why do you think it was important for Guru Nanak to be accompanied by his friend Mardana on his travels?

2 **a)** Why do you think people were challenged by Guru Nanak's message of equality?
   b) Why do you think some people found it difficult to sit down and eat in the free kitchen?

3 Guru Nanak set up a community so that his followers could 'work, learn and pray together'. Imagine that you want to get a group of people from different backgrounds to work together. What things would you do to encourage them to get on with each other?

Before he died Guru Nanak, the first Sikh Guru, appointed his disciple, Lehna, as his successor. Guru Nanak gave Lehna the name Angad, which means 'part of my body'. This was important because all the Sikh Gurus who came after Guru Nanak sometimes called themselves Nanak. This showed that they were being guided by the same spirit that was in Guru Nanak.

● Guru Angad (1504–1552 CE)

Guru Nanak was impressed by Lehna's **humility**, devotion and commitment to the teachings. Guru Angad taught that the best way to be saved was by performing one's worldly duties. He wrote many hymns and opened schools to teach the young. He believed in physical fitness and encouraged the disciples with exercise and competitive games, such as wrestling. He developed the free kitchen where everyone ate the same meal, with no one given a special place. He collected together the hymns of Guru Nanak. Guru Angad also developed the **Gurmukhi** script in which the hymns are written today in the **Guru Granth Sahib**.

● Guru Amar Das (1479–1574 CE)

Guru Angad said there was no difference between himself and Guru Amar Das. The new Guru was visited by the Emperor Akbar. The Emperor was asked to eat a meal seated on the floor with the other visitors, which he did. Guru Amar Das set up the twenty-two districts into which Sikhs were organised. He made the first day of Vaisakhi and Diwali special days when Sikhs gather together to celebrate. Guru Amar Das wrote the **Anand Sahib** which is said near the end of every service of worship.

▶ *Guru Amar Das*

Guru Ram Das (1534–1581 CE)

He was the son-in-law of Guru Amar Das. The name Ram Das means 'servant of God'. He spread the Sikh message by sending teachers to distant parts of the country. He wrote many hymns, and some are used at ceremonies such as marriage. During his time the Emperor Akbar helped get some land, which Guru Ram Das bought. The Guru lived there with his followers. He started to build a pool there and it became the place where Sikhs gathered for their festivals. This village later became known as **Amritsar**, the great centre of the Sikh faith.

◄ *The city of Amritsar surrounding the Golden Temple*

Guru Arjan Dev (1563–1606 CE)

He was the youngest son of Guru Ram Das. He completed the 'Tank' at Amritsar, and a temple was built in its centre. Today this is known as the Golden Temple or **Harimandir**. Disciples donated one-tenth of their income to pay for it. This was collected on the first day of Vaisakhi each year. Guru Arjan is most famous for collecting together the hymns of the first four Gurus and other writers. He added some of his own and these became the **Adi Granth**, which means first collection. These are the Sikh scriptures. He was concerned about the needs of those less fortunate and opened a leprosy centre. Emperor Jehangir persecuted the Sikhs and Guru Arjan became a **martyr** in 1606. He was roasted alive and his body was thrown in the river.

▲ *An early handwritten version of the Adi Granth*

Guru Hargobind (1595–1644 CE)

He was the only child of Guru Arjan. He carried out his father's wishes by wearing two swords, one representing spiritual power and the other authority over our mortal world. He trained the Sikhs to fight and constructed a fort at Amritsar. There were many clashes with the emperor's army and Guru Hargobind and his disciples had to withdraw to the mountains because they were outnumbered. His release from prison is celebrated at Diwali by Sikhs.

Guru Har Rai (1630–1661 CE)

Guru Har Rai was the grandson of Guru Hargobind. He tried to live in peace and spread Sikh teachings. The new emperor, Aurangzeb, was much less tolerant and this forced the Sikhs to withdraw even further into the mountains.

Guru Har Krishan (1626–1664 CE)

He was the second son of Guru Har Rai and was only five years old when he became Guru. He looked after those suffering from smallpox. Unfortunately, he caught the disease himself and died. He was the only Guru who was not married with a family.

Guru Tegh Bahadur (1621–1675 CE)

He was the fifth son of Guru Hargobind. His name means 'brave sword' and he earned it on the battlefield. He spent much time travelling, trying to encourage Sikhs. He took his mother and wife with him to emphasise that religion is concerned with the family. He wished to live in peace and feed the hungry. Emperor Aurangzeb persecuted those who did not share his beliefs. The Emperor threatened to kill the Brahmin Hindus. They turned to Guru Tegh Bahadur for protection. He told them to tell the Emperor that they would change their beliefs if Guru Tegh Bahadur could be converted. The Guru was beheaded when he could not be persuaded. He is especially important because he sacrificed his life for the beliefs of others; beliefs he did not share.

▲ *Guru Tegh Bahadur*

1 Write a sentence about the main achievement or contribution of the following to the Sikh faith: Guru Angad, Guru Amar Das, Guru Ram Das, Guru Arjan. In each case say why you have chosen that achievement.

2 **a)** What things do you think were considered when a new Guru was chosen? (Clues: were they all relatives? Were they young or old when they became Guru? What qualities did they have?)

b) What qualities do you think are needed by a Head Teacher?

c) What things do you think should be considered when choosing a new Head Teacher?

3 How did all the Gurus show that the spirit that guided Guru Nanak also guide them?

4 **a)** All the Gurus, except one, were married with families. How might this have affected their beliefs and what they taught?

b) What particular events changed the character of Sikhism?

5 **a)** Write down the meaning of the word 'martyr'.

b) Which Gurus were martyred and why?

c) How do you think these events affected the Sikhs?

6 It is important for Sikhs to stand up for the rights of others and care for them. Choose one thing that is important to you and explain why you would want to help, and suggest things that you could do to help.

Guru Gobind Rai (later called Guru Gobind Singh) was the only son of Guru Tegh Bahadur who had been martyred for defending the beliefs of others. It had been prophesied that Guru Gobind Rai would save humanity.

Emperor Aurangzeb had driven away anyone who challenged him or had different beliefs. The Sikhs, like other religious groups, were not happy. Guru Gobind Rai had the personality to change all this. He knew that his followers needed strong leadership and spiritual direction. He was a highly skilled soldier, but was also very clever and concerned about the rights of all people.

He needed to restore confidence and unite the people. He also needed to create a courageous people who would recognise the rights and needs of others, and would not see the differences of race, colour and religion. He trained the Sikhs to be soldiers; encouraging them to develop physical strength and mental toughness through sports.

He also wrote powerful poetry, which gave them spiritual strength. These poems talked of the supremacy of God, not of emperors . . .

> ● . . . God alone is the only Giver and Ruler of all. All stand like beggars at his court.
>
> *Guru Gobind Singh*

He restored the faith of all Sikhs in God and in themselves. As the Sikhs grew in confidence they were attacked by those who feared them. They stood firm.

Soon they joined with others who were opposed to Emperor Aurangzeb. The Emperor sent his son with an army to destroy the Sikhs, but they did not succeed. A period of peace followed. This gave Guru Gobind Rai the chance to strengthen the Sikh position.

11

◀ *A portrait of Guru Gobind Rai (Singh) in a gurdwara*

● Vaisakhi 1699

> ● It is through the actions of the Khalsa that I have won all my victories and have been able to give charity to others.
>
> *Guru Gobind Singh*

Large numbers of Sikhs had gathered to celebrate the festival of Vaisakhi in 1699 CE. Guru Gobind Rai wanted them to show unity and strength in those difficult times. This was to be no ordinary Vaisakhi.

Holding a sharp sword he asked for volunteers who would give their heads for him. After a long period one man came forward. The Guru led him into the tent and returned with his sword dripping with blood. Four more times he repeated the request, and four more times he appeared with his blood-soaked sword.

However, after the last time he returned with the five men, all unharmed. They had shown true devotion and trust in the Guru and his beliefs. They were the **Panj Pyares**, the 'five beloved ones' who formed the basis of the **Khalsa**, which means the pure community. It was, and is, a close-knit family of Sikhs.

The five were given a special mixture called **Amrit** to **initiate** them. Then they initiated the Guru and many others.

The Guru told them how they would be expected to behave in the future. He also laid down strict standards of dress and gave them new names. All men would be called 'Singh', which means lion, and all women 'Kaur' which means princess. These new Sikhs did not recognise differences of caste or religion.

> ● All men have the same eyes, ears, body and figure made out of the compounds of earth, air, fire and water.
>
> *Guru Gobind Singh*

▲ *Guru Gobind Singh calls for volunteers to give their heads for the Sikh faith*

▲ *Modern day Sikhs representing the Panj Pyares at a ceremony*

▲ *A picture in a gurdwara which shows Guru Gobind Singh compiling the Guru Granth Sahib*

The Guru was now known as Gobind Singh. He gathered the Sikhs and moved to meet Aurangzeb. They were going to talk about what the Emperor was doing to the Sikhs, but the Emperor died before they arrived. Guru Gobind Singh supported the Prince who had helped the Sikhs. He became Emperor Bahadur Shah. The Sikhs worked closely with him, but Guru Gobind Singh had made some enemies because he said it was right for all people to worship as they choose. On 7 October 1708 CE the Guru was stabbed to death by one of these enemies.

His final contribution to the Sikhs was to say that there would be no more human Gurus. In future the Guru would be the scriptures, known as the Guru Granth Sahib.

1 For each of the following write a sentence to explain the meaning: Khalsa, Panj Pyares, Singh, Kaur.

2 How did Guru Gobind Rai develop the confidence of the Sikhs?

3 Imagine you were present at Vaisakhi in 1699 CE. Write a letter to a friend describing the events, the Guru and your feelings at the time.

4 Read the three quotations in this chapter. They were all written by Guru Gobind Singh. What do they tell you about the things he believed in?

5 Guru Gobind Singh did many things for the Sikhs. Which one do you think was most important? Give your reasons.

- Waheguru ji ka Khalsa, Waheguru ji ki Fateh.

- The Khalsa belongs to the Lord, victory to the Lord.

The first members of the Khalsa, the Panj Pyares, had to show that they were willing to die for the Guru and their Sikh beliefs. Membership of this community was not planned to be an easy option, and not all Sikhs become members. Today, initiation as a member of the Khalsa is carried out in the same way that the Panj Pyares were initiated in 1699.

▲ *Sikhs in ceremonial dress*

Each member of the Khalsa adopts the name Singh or Kaur. The name Singh means lion and it describes how male Sikhs should behave and be treated. Like the lion they should be strong and fearless, but gentle and caring; they should be treated with respect. The name Kaur shows that women should be like princesses and be treated like them also. These are examples of the high standards expected of Sikhs.

Guru Gobind Singh also united Sikhs by giving the Khalsa **symbols** of their identity and strength. These are known as the **Panj Kakke** or 'Five Ks'. They must be worn by both male and female members of the Khalsa. Not all Sikhs wear them because not all Sikhs are initiated as members of the Khalsa. Each is an outward symbol of the inner beliefs of the Khalsa Sikh and their dual duty to be both saint and soldier.

● The Five Ks

The Five Ks are:

Kesh – uncut hair
Kangha – a comb
Kachha – shorts
Kara – a steel wristlet
Kirpan – a sword

● KESH

Sikhs believe that uncut hair, kesh, is a gift from God and is a sign of saintliness. To cut and shape the hair is a sign of human vanity. Uncut hair unites Khalsa Sikhs; it is a symbol of their difference and identity.

Kesh

● KANGHA

The comb is used to keep the long, uncut hair tidy. Sikhs must keep their hair clean, with regular washing and combing. The kangha is used to tie the hair up, thus making sure that it looks tidy. Men do not shave, and the beard is often tied neatly in a net. The rules of the Khalsa expect men to wear a turban.

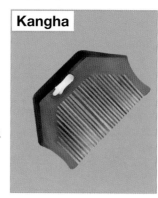

Kangha

● KARA

Kara

This is a plain steel band worn around the right wrist. It is a circle, without beginning or end. This reminds Sikhs that God is **eternal** and that they should do good deeds. The circle reminds them of the unity of the Khalsa. Steel is a sign of strength. Circles also protect, and this reminds Sikhs of their own freedom, and responsibility to defend others as well as themselves.

● KACHHA

Kachha

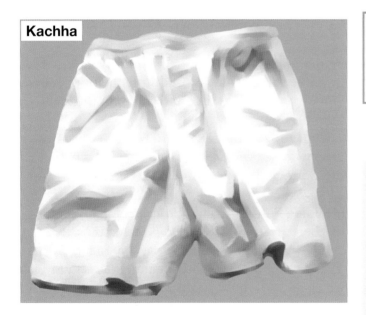

The shorts also remind Sikhs of their duty to others. They are underclothes worn by both men and women. Some say that they make fighting easier, so the Sikh is always ready to go into action, especially to help others. Other Sikhs say they are a constant reminder of the need for self control in all they do.

> ● To fight and accept death for a righteous cause is the privilege of the brave and truly religious.
>
> *Guru Nanak*

● KIRPAN

Kirpan

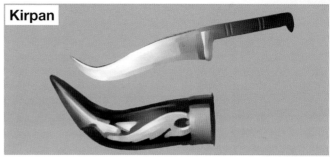

The sword is a symbol of freedom. Many of the Gurus fought battles to defend both Sikh and Hindu communities. Guru Hargobind wore two swords, to stand for the spiritual and worldly authority of the Guru. A sword reminds Sikhs of their duty to protect and defend the weak. In his letter to Emperor Aurangzeb, Guru Gobind Singh said:

> ● Do not mercilessly and ruthlessly use your sword on the helpless people . . .
> ● When all other means to curb tyranny fail, it is lawful to take up the sword.

1 In groups discuss how (i) a lion and (ii) a princess should behave and be treated. Share your ideas with other groups and write down an acceptable definition.

2 Khalsa men are given the name 'Singh' because they are expected to be lion-hearted. If you could be named after an animal, which would you choose and why?

3 **a)** What does Khalsa Sikh mean?
 b) How is a Khalsa Sikh different from other Sikhs?

4 **a)** Draw pictures of the Five Ks into your book.
 b) Write a short explanation, in your own words, of what you think each means to a Khalsa Sikh.

5 **a)** Write down some groups which expect their members to wear uniforms. What rules and standards of behaviour are expected?
 b) Make a poster showing the different groups and what is expected of the members.

6 Design a new school uniform. Explain why you have chosen the various parts, what they should mean to everyone who attends the school and how they will help everyone feel more like an important member of the school.

► *The Guru Granth Sahib is written in Gurmukhi script*

> ● He who wishes to behold the Guru, let him search the Holy Granth.
>
> *Guru Gobind Singh*

After the death of Guru Gobind Singh there were to be no more human Gurus. Instead Sikhs would be guided by their holy book, the Guru Granth Sahib.

It was Guru Arjan who gave the scriptures their form. He collected together the writings of the first four Gurus and added his own. He also included hymns written by Hindu and Muslim poets, as long as they agreed with Sikh teachings. This taught Sikhs that there is much to be learnt by listening to others.

> ● Without the true Guru, the path is not found.
>
> *Beni*

He placed the hymns in strict order, according to the thirty-one ragas or tunes to which they are sung. One of the ways the hymns were organised was to collect together those of each Guru.

The present Guru Granth Sahib is not exactly the same as the Adi Granth or First Collection of Guru Arjan. Guru Gobind Singh added some hymns written by Guru Tegh Bahadur, and even one of his own. Nevertheless, many Sikhs use the titles Guru Granth Sahib and Adi Granth to mean the same scriptures.

Today all copies of the Guru Granth Sahib are exactly the same as the original. They are written in the Gurmukhi script. This is used because the hymns were originally written in many different languages, including Punjabi, Hindi, Persian and Sanskrit.

There are 1,430 pages and 3,384 hymns. The same hymns are on the same page in each copy. There is an introduction containing the set prayers which are said in the morning, at dusk and at night. This is followed by the main collection of hymns which ends with those written by Hindus and Muslims. The names of some of the writers are Kabir, Namdev, Ravidas, Farid and Dhanna. Finally, there is a collection of hymns by various writers mainly in the form of **couplets**. The Gurus who have provided most of the hymns in the Guru Granth Sahib are, in order, Arjan, Nanak, Amar Das, Ram Das and Angad.

> ● Nanak, think always in your heart and mind on God's Name that at the last moment it may rescue you . . .
>
> *Guru Ram Das*

▲ *The Guru Granth Sahib is placed on a throne and is attended by a* **granthi**

Sikhs respect the Guru Granth Sahib very highly, but do not worship it. It is believed to be the Word of God, and Sikhs give it the same devotion and obedience that they gave the human Gurus.

It is given a position of honour in the place of worship, the **gurdwara**, and everyone sits at a level below it. It must be present at all important ceremonies. When it is moved all must stand, and it is carried on the head of a bearer, wrapped in clean decorated cloths. The uninterrupted reading of the Guru Granth Sahib is an important feature of festivals. It may also be taken in procession through the streets.

At home, Sikhs are expected to read through it. Many Sikh homes have a copy which is placed in a separate room called the gurdwara. However, not all Sikh homes have such a room as the Guru Granth Sahib must be kept in a high place of honour. In such homes the family will keep a **Gutka** containing extracts from the Guru Granth Sahib.

- We treat our Holy Book just like a living Guru. We respect it like a living Guru. It's given a special place in the gurdwara . . . above everyone else!

- It guides our lives. When I want advice I get someone to open it for me and the first paragraph on the page will give me the answer.

Showing respect to the Guru Granth Sahib.

It's given a position of honour. Everyone sits below it.

It is present at all important ceremonies.

People stand when it is moved. It is covered in a clean cloth and is carried on the head.

▲ *Ways of showing respect to the Guru Granth Sahib*

● **DASAM GRANTH**

The **Dasam Granth** or Tenth Collection is a separate scripture. It does not have the same importance as the Guru Granth Sahib and is not treated with the same amount of respect. It contains mainly the hymns and writings of the tenth Guru, Gobind Singh, one of which is his autobiography. The hymns were collected together by one of his disciples after the Guru's death. Many of them are about peace and harmony . . .

> ● All are the same, none is separate, a single form, a single creation.
>
> *Guru Gobind Singh*

Others reflect the hard times in which he lived . . .

> ● And when the time comes, I shall die, fighting heroically in battle.
>
> *Guru Gobind Singh*

1 Name three Gurus and three other poets whose writings are part of the Guru Granth Sahib.

2 Name three different languages in which the hymns of Guru Granth Sahib were composed.

3 What is the difference between the Adi Granth and the Guru Granth Sahib?

4 In what ways do Sikhs show respect to the Guru Granth Sahib?

5 Why do many Sikh households not have a copy of the Guru Granth Sahib? Why do you think it might be difficult to look after one properly in a modern house. Share your answers with others and note down the reasons given.

6 Design a room where it would be suitable and easy for a Sikh family to keep a copy of the Guru Granth Sahib. In what part of the house would this room have to be?

7 In groups discuss and note down how you show that something is of great importance to you. How do you treat it? How do you expect others to treat it? How would you protect it and look after it? Share your findings with other groups and draw up a list of all that you have discovered.

8 Read the quotations from and about the Sikh scriptures. In your own words write down what you think they say about the Sikhs and the respect they have for their Holy Book.

'Rahit' means conduct or discipline. When Guru Gobind Singh founded the Khalsa he had told them exactly how they should behave. For many years there had been disputes about what was in this code of conduct. Some of the very early versions of the code included ideas that the Guru would not have approved.

A special committee was set up to make the position clear. They worked for nearly fifteen years to produce a version that would be acceptable. This was published on 3 February 1945 and is known as the **Rahit Maryada**. Today it is often just called the 'Rahit'.

It was published by the Shiromani Gurdwara Parbandhak Committee (SGPC). This is the committee that is responsible for all the gurdwaras in Punjab. This committee is concerned with educating the Sikh people and helping them understand their faith more. The Rahit was originally written in Gurmukhi, but there is now a version in English. This is needed because many Sikhs now live in Britain, America and Canada.

The picture below shows the cover of the Rahit Maryada with the seal of the SGPC on it.

▲ Akal Takht, the main meeting place for the Shiromani Gurdwara Parbandhak Committee (SGPC)

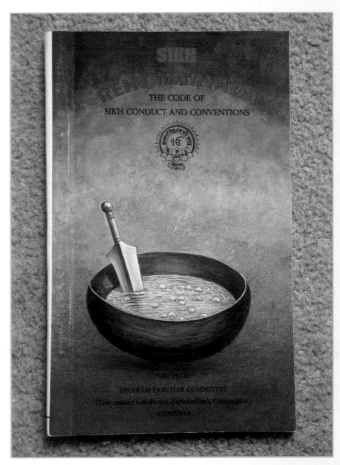

▲ Rahit Maryada bearing the seal of the SGPC

The introduction to the English version says:

- Reht Maryada may be taken as the key to Sikh spiritual and social philosophy.

It is divided into many sections. All parts of a Sikh's life are covered by the Rahit. It starts by saying that a Sikh is anyone who believes in:

one eternal God,
the Ten Gurus and their teachings,
the Guru Granth Sahib,
baptism by Amrit, and
is not a member of another religion

Then Rahit Maryada lays down what Sikhs are expected to do in their lives within the Sikh community and in the wider world. The need to meet with other Sikhs to think about and understand the **gurbani**, the teachings of the Guru Granth Sahib, is stressed.

- . . . it is necessary for a Sikh to visit the places where Sikhs congregate for worship and prayer (the gurdwaras), and joining the congregation, partake of the benefits that the study of the holy scriptures bestows.

    Rahit Maryada
    (with permission of SGPC)

▲ *Sikhs attending the gurdwara show they follow the Rahit Maryada; they listen to the teachings of the Gurus and benefit from the company of other Sikhs*

There are also lots of expectations about family life and life in the wider world. Here are some of them:

● FAMILY LIFE

- A Sikh should pray to God before launching off on any task.

- It is a Sikh's duty to get his children educated in Sikhism.

- A Sikh should keep the hair of his sons and daughters intact.

- A Sikh must not take hemp (cannabis), opium, liquor, tobacco, in short, any intoxicant.

- Piercing of nose or ears for wearing of ornaments is forbidden for Sikh men and women.

- It is not proper for a Sikh woman to wear a veil or keep her face hidden . . .

● WIDER WORLD

- The true Sikh . . . shall make an honest living by lawful work.

- A Sikh shall regard a poor person's mouth as the Guru's cash offerings box.

- A Sikh shall observe the rules of conduct . . . right up to the end of his life.

- A Sikh shall not steal . . . or engage in gambling.

- Voluntary service is a prominent part of Sikh religion.

Rahit Maryada
(by permission of SGPC)

Rahit Maryada is very important to Sikhs. Individual Sikhs and the community aim to achieve the standard that it sets for their lives.

▲ *Children are educated as Sikhs by learning to sing shabads (hymns from the Guru Granth Sahib)*

1 Write a sentence to explain each of the following: (i) Rahit Maryada (ii) SGPC.

2 a) Carefully read the quotations in this chapter.
   b) Write a paragraph to describe some of the ways in which Sikhs are expected to behave.

3 Choose three of the rules that Sikhs are expected to follow. Explain why you think that they are good things to do.

4 a) In groups draw up a list of ten rules that you think people need to obey in order to make life happier for everyone.
   b) On your own, write a paragraph to explain why these rules will make everyone happier.

Sikhism is especially concerned with how people think of and behave towards God. This is expressed in the way Sikhs live and behave. Below are the beliefs which are at the centre of the Sikh faith.

● God

> ● God is the beginning and end of everything. He is the Designer and Creator.
>
> *Guru Gobind Singh*

> ● God takes care of all, at all times, birds, beasts, mountains, snakes and kings. God loves all beings in the sea and on the land . . .
>
> *Guru Gobind Singh*

Sikhs believe that God is Truth. Their main beliefs about God are in the **Mul Mantra**, or basic prayer. It was written by Guru Nanak and is the opening section of the **Japji**. The Japji is the morning prayer said by Sikhs. It is at the beginning of the Guru Granth Sahib.

▲ *The Mul Mantra in Gurmukhi script*

The Mul Mantra can be translated as:

There is One God
Whose Name is Truth.
God is the Creator,
and is without fear and without hate.
God is timeless,
God's Spirit is throughout the universe.
God is not born,
Nor will die to be born again,
God is self-existent.
By the grace of the Gurus God is made known to mankind.

Sikhs believe that God's name is most important. It should be remembered, repeated and meditated upon at all times. The practices of Nam Japo (repeating the Name of God) and Nam Simaran (meditating on the Name of God) are important ways for Sikhs to worship God. The morning prayer, Japji, is a meditation on and repetition of the Name of God. Sikhs can do this by saying the Japji, repeating '**Waheguru**' (Wonderful Lord) or listening to hymns in the gurdwara. These are the most important ways that Sikhs show their love of God.

▶ *Ek Aum-kar; this means 'God is One'; it is the first line of the Mul Mantra*

> ● If you desire eternal happiness of all types devote yourself to God's Name.
>
> *Guru Gobind Singh*

22

● Guru

Having the right Guru is important to Sikhs. A guru is a religious teacher. Some people say that it is made from two words. Firstly there is 'gu', which means darkness, and then there is 'ru', light. A guru is someone who leads you from darkness into light. For Sikhs the right guru to show them the light is the Guru Granth Sahib. It contains the teachings of the human Gurus and shows Sikhs what God wants (God's Will). Sikhs must listen to the gurbani, the teaching of the Guru.

> ● Without a Guru no one has reached God, for all his talking; it is he who shows the way and teaches true devotion.
>
> *Guru Nanak*

Sikhs are guided by the Will of God in all they do. For example, the Guru Granth Sahib is often opened at the place that God guides and is read from the start of that section. This is known as **hukam**, which means an order (from God).

◀ *A hukam being read as the* **sangat** *sits and listens*

---

1 Write a sentence to explain each of the following: (i) Mul Mantra, (ii) Japji, (iii) hukam, (iv) Guru and (v) gurbani.

2 Carefully read the Mul Mantra. Write down, in your own words, what it says about God.

3 **a)** What are Nam Japo and Nam Simaran?

  b) Why are they important to Sikhs?

4 **a)** Why do Sikhs believe it is important to (i) have the right Guru, and (ii) follow the Will of God?

  b) Why do Sikhs believe that the Guru Granth Sahib is the right Guru?

Reincarnation and the Goal of Life

> • One who seeks pleasure wanders from birth to birth,
> Not caring about God's Will.
>
> *Guru Nanak*

> • There are connections between this life and the life lived previously. The soul doesn't die; it takes forward some small trace of what it behaved like in previous lives. The soul doesn't know, nor does the person you now are. This life gives you the chance to put right things you may have done wrong in previous lives. Then God might free you from rebirth . . . Only God knows when you will be reunited with God.
>
> • . . . those who fall at the feet of God and seek His protection shall not go through the cycle of being reincarnated.
>
> *Guru Gobind Singh*

Sikhs believe in reincarnation, which means being reborn. Those who are reborn have followed their own selfish ways. They may have ignored what God wants (God's Will). They might have been envious of others, not cared for others or been greedy.

Sikhs want to break free from being reborn. They want to be united with God. Freedom from being reborn is called 'mukti'. Mukti comes from the grace of God. A Sikh must be filled with God. He or she can do this by listening to the gurbani, meditating on the Name of God, repeating the Name of God and through worship. If these things are done then God might grant release from rebirth.

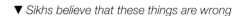
▼ *Sikhs believe that these things are wrong*

24

1 In groups write down (i) five examples of behaviour that you think might cause people to be reborn, and (ii) five examples of how God might want Sikhs to behave. Give reasons for the examples you have chosen.

2 Imagine that you are a Sikh. Write down ways in which you might be able to show that you are following God's Will in the whole of your life.

3 In groups draw up a list of people today whom you believe might be able to lead others from 'darkness to light'. Say what they believe in and what their worthwhile qualities are.

Birth

After a baby has been born, when the mother is well enough, the family go to the gurdwara. Usually at the end of the service a special ceremony takes place. The parents bring the baby to the front and stand before the Guru Granth Sahib. Special thanksgiving hymns are sung.

> ● God has sent this wonderful gift; conceived by grace may he live many years.
>
> *Guru Arjan*

The Guru Granth Sahib is opened at random, and the hymn is read. The name of the child must begin with the first letter of the hymn. The parents decide on the name and it is announced to everyone. The same names can be used for boys and girls, the only difference being in the common names Singh and Kaur.

The first five and last verses of the prayer Anand Sahib, a prayer of joy, are read. Then the whole of the **Ardas** is said. Finally **Karah Parshad** is distributed. This holy food will have been bought and often prepared by the family. Karah Parshad is made from equal amounts of sugar, water, butter and semolina or plain flour.

▲ *The Guru Granth Sahib has been opened at random*

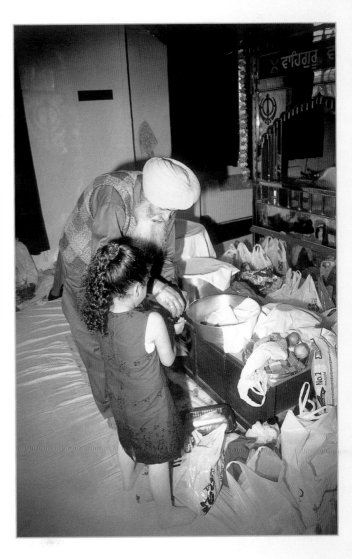

▶ *A young Sikh child receiving Karah Parshad*

There may be other parts to the ceremony. Sometimes a mixture of honey and water called Amrit is prepared. The Japji will then be recited. A kirpan may be dipped in the amrit and then lightly touched onto the baby's tongue. Amrit is the sacred mixture used at initiation, and this reminds all present of their Sikh duty to raise the child in the faith. It also emphasises the sweetness of the gurbani.

It is also a custom for the parents to present a gift to the gurdwara. This is often a new **romala**, decorated cloth, to cover the Guru Granth Sahib. A family may arrange for the Guru Granth Sahib to be read from beginning to end without a break. This is known as **Akhand Path**.

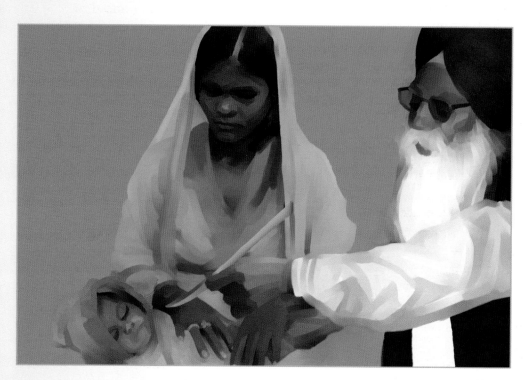

◀ *Amrit is placed on the tongue of the baby with the tip of a kirpan*

1 Copy out and complete this paragraph.
   After the birth of a baby, Sikh parents go to the _____. A _____ takes place and the baby is given a name. The baby is brought before the _____ _____ _____. A reading is chosen and the baby's name must begin with the _____ letter of the _____. The same names can be used for _____ and _____. At the end of the service the _____ is said.

2 What is (i) Karah Parshad, and (ii) Akhand Path?

3 Imagine you have been attended the naming of a Sikh baby. In your own words write a letter to a pen-friend describing what happened.

4 Do you think that it is important to have a special naming ceremony for a baby? Give reasons for your answer.

5 For what do you think that everyone present is giving thanks? How do you think that the ceremony shows this? How do you think the ceremony shows that parents are devoted to God?

6 **a)** What reasons do people have for choosing particular names? (Clue: why was your name chosen?)
   b) If you could make the choice now, what name would you choose for yourself and why?

● Amritsanskar – Initiation

This is the most important ceremony for Sikhs. It shows that a Sikh is ready to be fully committed to the Sikh faith. He or she becomes a member of the Khalsa, the Pure Community of Sikhs. Anyone who understands and is committed can go through the **Amritsanskar** ceremony.

The ceremony is similar to the initiation of the Panj Pyares on Vaisakhi 1699 CE. They are represented at the ceremony by five **amrit-dhari** Sikhs. These are Sikhs who have been through Amritsanskar. They wear the ceremonial saffron dress and the Five Ks.

The ceremony usually takes place in private, in the gurdwara. Another amrit-dhari Sikh is present to read from the Guru Granth Sahib.

The ceremony begins with the opening of the scriptures. Those wishing to be initiated are asked a number of questions:

● Are they willing to read, learn and live according to Sikh teachings?
● Will they pray only to the one God?
● Will they serve the whole of humanity?

When they have agreed, a prayer is said and a hukam is read from the scriptures.

The Amrit is now prepared. The sugar and water are mixed together in an iron bowl by the five amrit-dhari Sikhs. They kneel around the bowl and stir the Amrit with a double-edged sword. They say prayers including the Japji and verses from the Anand Sahib.

▲ *The **Khanda** is an important Sikh symbol. The double-edged sword is called a Khanda and is used to stir the Amrit*

The Ardas is said and the candidates come forward one by one to kneel by the bowl to receive Amrit. They are initiated by drinking a handful of Amrit. They do this five times, and each time they say:

● Waheguru ji ka Khalsa, Waheguru ji ki Fateh.

This can be translated as:

● The Khalsa is dedicated to God.
  The victory belongs to God.

◀ *A double-edged sword is used to stir the Amrit*

▲ *Amritsanskar – the initiation ceremony*

The Mul Mantra is said five times and the rules of the Khalsa are explained to the new members. The rules they must obey do not let them smoke or take drugs, eat meat which has been ritually slaughtered, commit adultery or cut their hair.

The ceremony ends with the saying of Ardas, a further reading from the Guru Granth Sahib and the sharing of Karah Parshad.

Members of the Khalsa are expected to set high standards. They should be willing to sacrifice themselves for others and not have any bad habits, such as gambling, telling lies or drinking alcohol. They should pursue peace, treat everyone equally, be optimistic, good tempered, earn money honestly and share it with the needy.

Not all Sikhs become members of the Khalsa. Those who do are known as amrit-dhari, because they have taken Amrit. Some Sikhs may wear their hair uncut and keep some of the rules of the Khalsa, although they have not been initiated. They are known as **kesh-dhari**, because they do not cut their hair. Many may worship regularly but not keep the Five Ks and the other standards. These people are known as sahaj-dhari because they are learning about the Sikh faith and are trying to follow its teaching, but they do not carry its symbols. There are other people who were born as Sikhs but do not practise their religion.

1 Write a sentence to explain each of the following: (i) amrit-dhari, (ii) kesh-dhari, and (iii) sahaj-dhari.

2 Look at the pictures which show the Amritsanskar ceremony taking place. Carefully read the section on Amritsanskar. Write a sentence to describe each picture accurately.

3 Look at the rules that members of the Khalsa are expected to obey. Which ones would you find easy? Which ones would you find difficult? Give your reasons.

4 The Amritsanskar ceremony is very similar to the original ceremony held in 1699 CE. Why do you think it is important that this ceremony is like the original?

5 Why do you think that most people think it is important to have a special ceremony when you become a full member of a group? How do you think that the ceremony helps (i) the person becoming a member, (ii) the group the person is joining, and (iii) others who are not members?

◀ *A girl reading her Nit nem in the Golden Temple. As well as the set times, Sikhs are encouraged to pray when they feel it is appropriate*

Prayers must be said at home in the morning, evening and last thing at night. These are set prayers known as **Nit nem**, the 'daily rule'. Sikhs learn Gurmukhi so that they can say the prayers and read the scriptures.

> ● We pray to try and make us more like the Gurus set out in the Guru Granth Sahib. It is when we give time to the Guru . . . we say our gurbani. In the morning we say the Japji and some other prayers. In the evening we recite **Rehiras**. Last thing at night we say **Sohilla**. We shouldn't ask for things for ourselves. Each time we end by saying Ardas, and asking for our sins to be forgiven, and for everything to be good for everyone. We believe if the Guru wants, he can make things happen.

Any time is a good time to read a hukam, but Sikhs will try to read one from the scriptures first thing in the morning. Sikhs also try to read through the scriptures on a regular basis.

Every Sikh home tries to have a special place set aside for the Guru Granth Sahib. Sometimes modern houses make it difficult to make sure that the Holy Book is treated properly. Sikhs would be very upset if they showed any disrespect to the

Guru Granth Sahib. This means that some Sikh homes will not have a complete copy of the scriptures.

Some Sikhs may have a Gutka, which is a smaller collection of hymns. It is also treated with respect and daily readings are made from it.

Sikhs learn about their faith at home and in the gurdwara. They can find out about other religions too. They try to make sure they do not offend members of other faiths. However, they must not get involved with any superstitions, such as wearing a good luck charm.

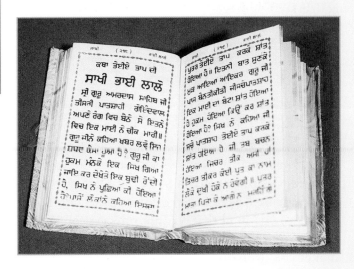

▲ *The Gutka – a collection of hymns from the Guru Granth Sahib*

Serving others is one of the highest ideals. Service is known as **seva**. It can be divided into three different types:
- intellectual (using your mind)
- manual (physical work)
- material (giving things).

Material service is the most common. Many people give money or things to charity, for example, raising funds for victims of natural or other disasters. Intellectual service can include explaining or teaching about Sikhism, or being a member of the gurdwara committee. Manual service could be cooking and serving food in the langar in the gurdwara. Service should not just be to Sikhs. It should include people from different religions and cultures, since Sikhs should treat all people as their brothers and sisters.

- When you become a member of the Khalsa you have to show everyone you love them. You do this by doing things to help them, by caring.

- It's important for all people to share in doing all sorts of jobs. We don't believe in the caste system, so it's right for somebody who is rich or clever to do ordinary things, like cooking and serving food in the langar.

- No work should be below anyone's dignity . . . if you need a volunteer for any job every Sikh should step forward . . . it's an honour to serve others.

◀ *A young Sikh performing seva in the langar*

▼ *Food is prepared so as not to offend anyone*

Although many Sikhs are vegetarian, they are allowed to eat meat that has not been killed in a religious ritual. When in the company of others, Sikhs provide food that will not offend people, so vegetarian food is normally chosen. Anything that makes you drunk or lose self-control should be avoided. Therefore Sikhs should not drink alcohol.

Sikhs should dress modestly. The combination of shalwar (baggy trousers) and kameez (tunic) is popular with women. This is sometimes called a Punjabi suit. All Khalsa Sikhs must wear the Five Ks. These can be worn with most styles of dress.

Hair should not be cut and can be kept tidy using the kangha or comb. Many Sikhs wear a turban. The turban is of great religious importance because the Guru Granth Sahib says that 'Only with the turban on is the appearance complete.' The turban was worn by all of the Sikh Gurus. Therefore, under the Race Relations Act, those Sikhs who wear turbans do not have to wear a crash helmet when riding a motorcycle.

Wearing a kirpan, or sword, has caused some difficulties. So it is kept in its sheath and is normally worn under the clothes during the day. Some Sikhs wear a small kirpan set into their kangha (comb) or on a necklace. However, this is not acceptable to Khalsa Sikhs.

> ● Sikhism is a practical religion; wearing the Five Ks is essential. Everyone can see me and know what I believe and stand for. It shows what I really think is important. If somebody said I couldn't wear them, I don't know what I'd do.

◀ *Young Sikhs with their teachers, all in traditional dress*

1 Write a sentence to explain what the following are:
(i) Nit nem, Rehiras, Sohilla, (ii) shalwar, kameez.

2 Why do Sikhs pray?

3 a) Explain why service is so important to Sikhs.
b) Design and produce a poster to show different ways that either intellectual or manual service can be performed. You should try to recommend service as a good way of spending leisure time.

4 Sikh women may choose not to wear make-up or jewellery. Why do you think this might be? What jewellery might a Sikh wear?

5 Why do you think that wearing the Five Ks has caused problems for some Sikhs?

6 Imagine that you are going to hold a party for some friends. How would you make sure that the food you prepared and the things that you planned to do did not offend any of them?

> Study of and meditation on the scriptures within the congregation is very important, and Sikhs should visit the gurdwara as often as possible.
>
> *Rahit Maryada*

The word gurdwara means 'the door to the Guru'. 'Dwara' means door or gate, while the Guru is the scriptures. It is the place where the gurbani or teachings of the Gurus can be studied, heard and meditated upon.

Gurdwaras differ in shape and size, but they all have a tall saffron (yellow) flag outside. The flag is tied tightly to the flag pole and the only part that can be seen shows the symbol of the Khalsa. It is called the Khanda. It takes its name from the double-edged sword in the centre. The flag is called the **Nishan Sahib**. Gurdwaras are visible from a long way off because of the Nishan Sahib. It also plays an important part in many of the festivals and other important occasions.

Before you get too far inside the gurdwara you have to take off your shoes and leave them in a special place. Shoes are not allowed in the main worship hall, or in many other parts! You must also cover your head. There may also be a notice telling you not to take tobacco or alcohol in with you. These actions show respect, and also that you are leaving the everyday world behind.

Inside, the worship hall is often large, but plain. There may be some pictures of the Gurus, but these are not worshipped.

The focus of attention is at the front. There stands the **palki** in which the Guru Granth Sahib is placed to show respect. In the centre of the palki is a raised platform or stool called the manji where the Guru Granth Sahib rests on cushions. When it is not open to be read it is covered by beautifully embroidered romalas. There is a canopy, called a chandni, above it. This may be decorated with streamers and gold and silver tinsel. The area where the Guru Granth Sahib rests is known as the **takht**, the throne.

▲ *The Nishan Sahib on the outside of the gurdwara makes it easily visible*

▲ *Inside the **diwan** (worship) hall of a gurdwara*

Someone often stands respectfully in attendance behind the scriptures waving a chauri, like a soldier on guard. The chauri is a fan made from hair. It is a symbol of authority. A granthi, who reads from the Guru Granth Sahib, sits just behind and slightly below it.

▲ The granthi is reading from the Guru Granth Sahib. The chauri can be seen beside him

The Guru Granth Sahib is treated with the greatest respect. There is always a room where it is laid to rest at night. This is usually a private room high in the gurdwara. It contains a bed which is covered with romalas. At the end of the day everyone stands as the granthi faces the Guru Granth Sahib and says the Ardas and reads a hukam. The scriptures are carefully wrapped in clean cloth. The head of the granthi is also covered with another clean cloth. The Guru Granth Sahib is placed on the granthi's head. Another person walks

behind waving the chauri. In this way the Guru Granth Sahib is taken to its resting place for the night. Next morning it will be returned to the takht in the same way.

▲ The Guru Granth Sahib being taken from the Golden Temple at night to its place of rest

There may be several other rooms inside the gurdwara. Some may be used for meetings or the committee which runs the gurdwara. There may also be schoolrooms, a library, a museum and rooms for the community to meet. People called gianis are responsible for the teaching. They, and the granthi, may have their own private living rooms in the gurdwara.

1 a) Copy and complete the grid, using the clues opposite.

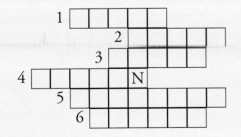

1 The canopy
2 A random reading
3 The raised platform
4 _____ Sahib (the flag)
5 The door to the Guru
6 The horse-hair fan

b) Copy the word which goes down the middle and give its meaning.

c) Draw the symbol in your books.

2 Using the picture above to help you, draw and label a plan of the worship hall.

3 What words would you choose to describe the worship hall in the photograph?

● Worship

There is no set day for diwan or worship. It takes place most days. The main day for meeting in Britain is Sunday, because this is when most people do not work.

▲ The ragis in the gurdwara. The instruments played will include drums and harmonium. A harmonium is a keyboard instrument similar to a pipe organ, but much smaller

▲ Worshippers bow and make offerings before joining the sangat

Worshippers enter the worship hall, approach the takht, bow and make an offering in a special box. Everyone sits on the floor with crossed legs. Feet must not point towards the Holy Book, as this would be very disrespectful. Men and women often sit apart, but do not have to do so.

Diwan consists mainly of **kirtan**, which is singing hymns from the Guru Granth Sahib. The **ragis** or singers do this and play musical instruments. While they do this the congregation meditates. Often the ragis explain the meaning of the hymn before they sing it. There may also be talks about Sikh teachings or history. This worship enables the congregation or sangat to repeat the Name of God and meditate upon it. By hearing the hymns the congregation are listening to the gurbani or teachings of the Gurus.

Before the worship the Karah Parshad, the holy sweet, will have been prepared and brought into the diwan hall. It is made from equal parts of sugar, water, butter and semolina or plain flour. It is placed near to the Guru Granth Sahib.

At the end of the service the Anand Sahib is said. This is followed by the part of the Japji which says . . .

> ● Our right and wrong acts shall be judged at Thy court. Some will be seated near Thy seat; some will be kept distant for ever.
> The toils have ended of those that have worshipped Thee,
> O Nanak, their faces are lit with radiant joy, many others they set free.

Everyone then stands and faces the Guru Granth Sahib and the granthi says the prayer Ardas. There is a final reading. The prayer asks for God to accept the Karah Parshad as sacred food for the congregation. The Karah Parshad is also touched with a kirpan. A small portion is set aside for the granthi and then the remainder is shared by all those present. It is a sign that the congregation accepts the equality of all people.

The Langar

> ● Let all share equally; no one should be seen as an outsider.
>
> *Guru Arjan*

A langar is a free kitchen. The first langar was set up by Guru Nanak. The main aim was to ensure that people from all backgrounds should eat together. This showed their commitment to equality. It also made sure that those who had travelled a long way to hear him, or were not very wealthy, could be given some food and drink.

By the time of Guru Amar Das, visitors were expected to share a meal before meeting together for prayer. Everyone ate the same food and there were no special places for anyone. Everyone was treated in exactly the same way, from an emperor to a poor person. People were also needed to prepare the food. This stressed the importance of serving others for Sikhs.

The langar in a modern gurdwara follows the same pattern. While the diwan takes place in the main worship hall, others are working in the langar. The kirtan is often relayed to the langar using loudspeakers so that everyone can take part.

Food is prepared for all the people attending the diwan. The meal is usually vegetarian to make sure that it causes no offence. The prayers said at the end of the diwan bless the meal. It is served to everyone. Often the meal is eaten standing up or sitting on the floor, to emphasise that everyone is treated equally.

There are always many volunteers to prepare and serve the meal. In fact, most gurdwaras have a long waiting list of families who want to pay for, cook and serve the meal. It is a custom for a family to share happy occasions with the whole community by serving in the langar. It is not surprising to find the local doctor or business owner serving in the langar. This is because seva is very important to Sikhs.

All visitors to a gurdwara are offered food and drink, so if you visit one expect to be offered something. It is bad manners to say no. It is not unusual for people who live on the streets to be aware of this and use the local gurdwara and langar as a place to obtain food and drink.

Sikhs do not turn anyone away, but do expect that everyone who shares the food undertakes some form of seva. People who just come for food are discouraged.

▲ *Everyone sits to eat at the same level to show that they are all equal*

1 Write a sentence to explain each of the following: (i) diwan, (ii) kirtan, (iii) ragis, (iv) langar.

2 In what ways to Sikhs show respect to the Guru Granth Sahib in the gurdwara?

3 In groups design a plan for a new gurdwara. Draw it on a large sheet of paper and mark the different parts that should be included.

4 Imagine that you have been on a visit to a gurdwara. Describe your visit in a letter to a pen-friend.

5 How does the langar help Sikhs to express their belief in serving the whole community?

6 In groups discuss and note down ways you could do things at school that would fulfil the Sikh belief in serving the whole community. Share your ideas with the rest of the class and see if there is any way you can actually carry out some of your ideas.

Sikhs have special ways of celebrating. The Guru Granth Sahib is central in many of these. One way of celebrating a festival or other important occasion is to have an Akhand Path. This is the reading of the Guru Granth Sahib from beginning to end without stopping. It takes about forty-eight hours and is done by a team of readers. It begins two days before and ends on the morning of the important day.

Before the reading the Anand Sahib and Ardas are said to ask for God's blessing on the occasion. Then a hukam is read. Karah Parshad is prepared and is available for visitors throughout the reading. It ends with the Anand Sahib, Ardas and the sharing of the holy food.

The Guru Granth Sahib may also be taken in procession through the streets of a town or city. In Britain a takht and palki may be set up on the back of a lorry, just like in the gurdwara. The Guru Granth Sahib is ceremoniously placed on the lorry.

Then it is driven slowly through the streets. As they go, five Khalsa Sikhs in ceremonial dress representing the Panj Pyares walk in front. Often hundreds of people follow behind.

▲ *The granthi is completing the reading of the Akhand Path*

- Sat siri Akal!
  Victory to the True Lord!

36

▶ *A special 'gurdwara' containing the Guru Granth Sahib is taken in procession through a city in Britain. In front of it walk five Khalsa Sikhs representing the Panj Pyares. Often thousands of Sikhs follow behind and line the route*

At other times the Nishan Sahib plays an important part. The flag is taken down and the flag pole is washed in water and yoghurt. Then the flag is replaced. The ceremony begins and ends with the Anand Sahib and Ardas. Hymns are sung by the congregation. The old flag is often torn up and those present treasure any piece they are able to collect.

The Gurus encouraged Sikhs to take part in sports and these are often part of the celebration. There are team games such as hockey and football. Individual events like wrestling, running, martial arts, badminton, table tennis and trials of strength are also common.

▲ *Other ways of celebrating may include bhangra dancing*

Bhangra dancing is very popular. Dancers dress in loose, brightly coloured costumes. It is very energetic. The dancing is accompanied by a person playing a large, narrow double-sided drum called a dhole. The dancers may twirl sharp swords as they dance, making it very spectacular. There may also be a fair. The sideshows and attractions vary between countries.

▲ *The Nishan Sahib is taken down, the flag removed and the pole washed in water and yogurt*

1 Copy and complete the following paragraph:
At the _____ of many Sikh celebrations is the Guru Granth Sahib. One of the important ways of celebrating is to have an _____ _____. This is a non-stop reading of the Holy Book which takes about _____ hours to complete. Anand Sahib and _____ are said at the beginning and end. Also _____ _____ is made and shared during, and at the end of the reading.

2 In what other ways is the Guru Granth Sahib shown to be important in Sikh celebrations?

3 In groups make a list of reasons why you think Sikhs make the Guru Granth Sahib the centre of their celebrations. Share your ideas with other groups.

4 Describe two other ways in which Sikhs might celebrate. Draw a picture of one of them.

5 Have you ever taken part in a public procession? If so, how did you feel?

6 What are the good things about taking part in sports activities?

Most Sikh festivals are gurpurbs or anniversaries of the Gurus. The word 'purb' means day, so these are days associated with a Guru. From the table below you can see that there are four main gurpurbs. Two celebrate births, and at two martyrdoms of Gurus are remembered. Others are related to events in the lives of Gurus. In the past dates were set by the Indian calendar, but the dates for most of the festivals have been agreed since 1999.

Most of these celebrations include a normal diwan and an Akhand Path. There may be a procession of the Guru Granth Sahib to remember the birth of Guru Nanak. Hymns composed by the Guru are sung in the gurdwara and there may be talks about his life. Similar events mark the birthday of Guru Gobind Singh. Hymns from the Dasam Granth will be used.

The martyrdoms of Guru Arjan and Guru Tegh Bahadur usually take place in the gurdwara. Hymns written by the Guru are sung. Sikhs may also hear talks about their importance to Sikhism.

FESTIVAL	ENGLISH CALENDAR DATE
Birth of Guru Nanak	November
Birth of Guru Gobind Singh	5 January
Hola Mahalla	14 March
Vaisakhi	14 April
Martyrdom of Guru Arjan	16 June
Martyrdom of Guru Tegh Bahadur	24 November
Diwali	October/November

▲ The main Sikh festivals

● Vaisakhi

▲ A poster advertising many of the events that were to take place at Vaisakhi for the 300th anniversary of the Khalsa

Vaisakhi is the most important Sikh festival. It is the birthday of the Khalsa. It is also the Sikh New Year.

The Nishan Sahib is replaced and there is a procession of the Guru Granth Sahib. In Britain it is usually on the Sunday following 14 April, but celebrations may carry on beyond that. It is one of the important days on which Guru Amar Das told Sikhs to gather together. Unity, courage and strength are remembered. So, team and individual sports are often played at Vaisakhi time. There may also be bhangra dancing, a fair and an exhibition of Sikh life. Often, at this time, there may be an Amritsanskar ceremony.

Diwali

This festival is also celebrated by Hindus. For Sikhs Diwali is different. It is the second day when Sikhs were told to gather together by Guru Amar Das. They remember the release from prison and return to Amritsar of Guru Hargobind. According to tradition he would only leave prison if fifty-two Hindu princes who were in prison with him could go free. The emperor at that time said that those who clung on to the Guru's coat could go free. All fifty-two left, hanging on to the tassles of Guru Hargobind's coat! So Diwali is a celebration of freedom and human rights.

There is kirtan in the gurdwara and talks about the Guru's life. There are firework displays and festive lights or divas (small oil lamps) are lit. Special meals are eaten.

▲ *Sikhs light candles at Diwali to remember the release of Guru Hargobind*

Hola Mahalla

Hola Mahalla is a spring festival, but it is of fairly minor importance. It was started by Guru Gobind Singh. It was originally a time for military exercises and training. Today it is mainly celebrated in the Punjab. Few people celebrate it in Britain.

1 What are the two days when Sikhs were told to gather together? Who told them this? At what time of the year do they take place?
2 Match the name of the festival with the correct reason for celebrating:

Festival	Reason for celebration
Hola Mahalla	birth of the Khalsa
Gurpurbs	spring festival
Vaisakhi	freedom
Diwali	anniversaries of the Gurus

3 Make a similar chart of all the festivals you celebrate each year, with your reasons for celebrating them.
4 Diwali and Vaisakhi were both important Hindu festivals. How have Sikhs made them Sikh celebrations?
5 Look at the picture of the poster on page 38. Choose one of the other festivals and design a poster advertising some of the celebrations which are to take place. It should be illustrated and encourage people to attend.

▲ *Guru Hargobind being released with the fifty-two princes holding on to the tassels of his cloak*

● Marriage

All the Gurus except one who died young were married. The love of the worshipper for God is likened to the love of the husband and wife for each other.

> ● Listen Lord-Spouse, this soul is lonely in the wilderness!
>
> My Beloved . . . how may I find peace without Thee?
> *Guru Nanak,* Guru Granth Sahib

Marriages are usually arranged. It is the joining of two families who should get on well. When the time is right for a young person to be married the family is consulted. Background, education and interests are taken into account.

Possible partners must be acceptable to each other and photographs are often exchanged. This is a quote from a Sikh woman about her marriage:

> ● It wasn't so much arranged as agreed. Other members of the family knew me in ways I didn't know myself. I might have made a bad choice – for the wrong reasons. No, I don't have any regrets – they were right!

▲ *The families meet and exchange gifts at the Milni before the ceremony*

A **betrothal** ceremony may be held. The girl's parents may present a kirpan and sweets for the boy as a commitment of both families to the marriage.

Marriage is called Anand Karaj, the ceremony of bliss. It takes place at the bride's home or nearby gurdwara. Marriage must take place in the presence of the Guru Granth Sahib.

Before the ceremony starts, members of both families meet, sing hymns and exchange gifts. This is known as the Milni.

▲ *The bride and groom sit before the takht. They are married in the presence of the Guru Granth Sahib*

The groom sits facing the takht, wearing a special scarf. The bride sits on his left. She may wear a shalwar, kameez and scarf of red and gold. These are the colours of happiness. The bride and groom are told about the responsibilities of marriage and given practical advice.

> ● Your family is where you learn about life . . . I love my parents and I knew they wouldn't do anything to hurt me; so when they said I should get married I didn't want to let them down, even though I wanted my own career . . . I never imagined I'd be this happy; now my husband is more important to me than my career.

The couple and their parents stand as a prayer is said to bless them. They all bow towards the Guru Granth Sahib to show they agree to the marriage. The bride's father puts garlands of flowers over the couple. He places one end of the groom's scarf in the bride's hands. She holds this scarf until the end of the ceremony.

Guru Amar Das said:

> ● They are not husband and wife who only live together. True husband and wife are those who have one spirit in two bodies.

The Lavan, the Marriage Hymn written by Guru Ram Das, is read. It says that growing love in marriage, and living by the teachings of the Gurus, will help the couples to be united with each other and God.

Each of the four verses is read separately. At the end of each verse the couple walk round the Guru Granth Sahib, keeping it to their right-hand side. As they complete each round they bow to the Guru Granth Sahib to accept its teaching. After the final round they may be showered with flower petals to show the joy of the occasion.

▲ *Each time a verse from the Lavan is read, the couple walk round the Guru Granth Sahib and then bow towards it to show that they agree to the teaching*

The newly-weds are welcomed by the bride's parents with sweets and garlands. Finally the congregation come forward and offer their congratulations. Gifts of money are placed in their laps to make sure that they have a good financial start to their married life. Everyone then leaves to share a meal.

1 In the word search below are a number of words connected to the Sikh marriage ceremony. Write down each one you can find. Then write a sentence to explain each one.

B	A	M	O	N	E	Y	K	J	L
N	E	O	K	C	S	B	A	P	A
A	N	G	A	R	L	A	N	D	V
V	L	J	F	D	K	D	A	R	H
A	M	I	N	M	A	I	S	V	P
L	K	V	I	H	D	L	C	A	M
M	I	L	A	V	G	E	A	L	I
A	N	A	N	D	K	A	R	A	J
I	L	R	M	R	E	J	F	K	V
A	K	V	D	K	L	I	O	J	A

2 a) In groups discuss the main features of the Sikh marriage ceremony.

   b) On your own choose six important points. Draw pictures to represent the various parts of the ceremony you have chosen. Underneath each picture write a caption to describe and explain what is happening.

3 What parts of the marriage ceremony show marriage is about the joining of two families?

4 In groups discuss whether there are any ways your family and friends know you better than you know yourself. Note the ideas you have. Share them with the rest of the class and see whether you agree or disagree with these ideas.

5 Most Sikhs are very keen to involve other members of the family in the choice of a marriage partner. What do you think are the advantages and disadvantages of this?

Funerals

> ● Each day that dawns must reach its end; All must leave, for none may stay.
> Our friends take their leave, we must also go. Death is our fate, our journey long.
>
> *Ravidas*, Guru Granth Sahib

> ● Man is proud of physical strength, wealth . . .
> None of these shall be his in death.
>
> *Guru Nanak*

Sikhs are taught to accept death as inevitable. Those who lose a loved one turn to the Guru Granth Sahib for support.

If a person is dying, then, if possible, the gurbani should be recited at his or her side. When a person has died, the body is washed and dressed in clean clothes. If the person was a Khalsa Sikh then the Five Ks will be worn.

The body should then be cremated. In Britain a crematorium is used. Before going to the crematorium, a service would be held in the gurdwara. Friends and relatives in the community can pay their last respects.

The body is then taken to the crematorium. As the body is being taken to be cremated hymns from the Guru Granth Sahib are sung. Ardas is said before the body is put into the fire. The funeral **pyre** should be lit by the son or a close relative. The congregation sit a distance away and listen to or recite the gurbani. When the pyre is well alight, Sohilla, the evening prayer, and Ardas are recited. Often the ashes are collected and placed in flowing water, though they can be buried.

Mourning lasts for up to ten days. This takes place at home or in a gurdwara. A reading of the Guru Granth Sahib starts with the Anand Sahib, Ardas and the sharing of Karah Parshad. The Guru Granth Sahib is read daily until it is completed during the time of mourning. Those who attend listen to the teachings of the Gurus and share Karah Parshad to support those who have lost a loved one.

The final prayers include this verse:

> ● When I am gone sing only those hymns which lead the devoted ones to blissful deliverance.
>
> *Sundar*

The period of mourning ends with the sharing of Karah Parshad for all those present.

▲ *There is a story about Guru Nanak's death which helps to show his belief that all people are equal. Even in death Guru Nanak did not show any favouritism to Hindu or Muslim followers*

◄ *A Sikh funeral*

There are no memorial stones or monuments to remember the person who has died. A hymn which is sometimes sung at Sikh funerals shows why.

The dawn of a new day
Is the herald of a sunset,
Earth is not our permanent home.
Life is like a shadow on a wall.

1 Look at the pictures of Guru Nanak's death on page 42.

   a) Describe what is happening in each picture.

   b) How does the story show that even after death Guru Nanak believed that there 'is neither Hindu nor Muslim'?

2 Write a paragraph to describe and explain what happens at a Sikh funeral.

3 Look carefully at the picture of the Sikh funeral. Why do you think the bier (a carriage or frame for carrying a dead body) is so brightly decorated?

4 **a)** Why do you think that Sikhs turn to the Guru Granth Sahib for comfort after someone has died?

   b) Who might you turn to for comfort at a time of great sadness? Can you think of an example? (You do not have to write this down or share it unless you want to.)

5 Carefully read the quotations in the section on death. In pairs discuss and write down what they tell you about how Sikhs feel about death.

6 Explain why you think that Sikhs do not believe in monuments for people who have died. Do you think that such monuments or memorials are a good idea? Give your reasons.

▲ *A sunset is the end of day, so death is the end of life*

● Amritsar

▲ *Harimandir (the Golden Temple), surrounded by the beautiful Holy Pool*

Amritsar means 'pool of nectar'. It is built on land that Guru Ram Das bought after the Emperor Akbar persuaded the owner to sell. It is in the Punjab in India.

Amritsar was known as Chak Ramdas or Ramdaspur, because it was Guru Ram Das who began building there in 1573 CE. A natural pool was there already, but Guru Ram Das wanted to make it bigger so that Sikhs could bathe there. The small pool became a large tank.

His youngest son, Guru Arjan, continued with the building. He made the tank more permanent. He also built the temple that stands in the middle of the tank. This is known as the Harimandir or temple of God. Its foundation stone was laid by a **devout** Muslim in 1589, after the tank was finished. The temple was completed in 1601 and the Adi Granth was put there in 1604.

Harimandir Sahib became known as the Golden Temple because it was covered by sheets of gold. Much of the beautiful art work on the ceilings and doors is also gold. Today Sikhs call it Darbar Sahib which means 'the court of the Lord'.

Sikh places of worship are not really temples because there is no image of God and sacrifices do not take place there. At Harimandir Sahib kirtan, diwan and langar are held in other buildings within the boundaries of the area.

The Golden Temple is built so that worshippers have to step down to enter it. This emphasises the need for humility before God. There are also doors on all four sides, to show that Sikhism is open to all people.

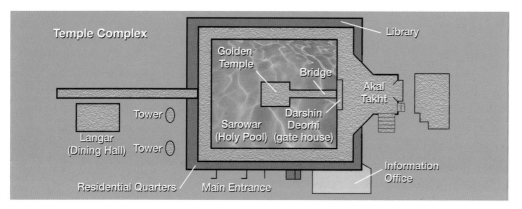

Temple Complex

Golden Temple

Bridge

Library

Akal Takht

Tower

Tower

Langar (Dining Hall)

Sarowar (Holy Pool)

Darshin Deorhi (gate house)

Residential Quarters

Main Entrance

Information Office

◄ *Plan of the area around Harimandir (the Golden Temple) at Amritsar*

There are two storeys and it is beautifully decorated. The building has lots of black and white marble with patterns made of precious stones. There are writings from the scriptures on the walls. The beauty of the building is spiritually uplifting for worshippers.

On the ground floor there is a takht, palki and a rail to guide the many worshippers around the Guru Granth Sahib. Ragis ceaselessly sing hymns and play music. On the upper floor the Guru Granth Sahib is read all the time. There is a small hall of mirrors to make the walls more beautiful and to show how important the Guru Granth Sahib is. In the past only a great emperor could have afforded a hall of mirrors. The Temple is 'crowned' by the golden dome.

As in all gurdwaras worshippers remove their shoes and cover their heads. They must wash their feet before entering the outer area. They bow as they enter Harimandir, leave gifts inside the rail and receive Karah Parshad as they leave. Many will also visit the nearby museum containing many important artefacts of the Sikh faith.

Below are the feelings of two Sikhs after visiting the Golden Temple.

● When I went to the Golden Temple I felt really happy. It was like being close to God.

● Just being there, I felt . . . at peace . . . contented . . . it made me feel good inside.

▲ *Inside Harimandir the Guru Granth Sahib is attended by a granthi as visitors pay their respects*

1 Explain the meaning of the following words:
(i) Harimandir and (ii) Darbar Sahib.

2 a) Who was the Guru when Harimandir was built?
b) Why is the Harimandir also known as the Golden Temple?

3 How does the building of Harimandir show that it is open to everyone and that they must be humble before God?

4 Explain why it is not really correct to call a Sikh place of worship a temple.

5 Imagine you are a Sikh visiting the Golden Temple for the first time. Write a letter to your family at home telling them about your visit. You should include what you saw, how you felt, etc.

6 Have you ever felt 'at peace . . . contented' in a special place? If so, explain where this was and why it made you feel like this.

7 a) How would you describe the Golden Temple from the photograph?
b) What is the most beautiful place you have ever visited? Can you find a picture of it and fix it in your workbook?

● The Five Takhts

The word takht usually means throne. The Five Takhts are places of spiritual authority. Many important religious decisions at a local level may be taken by a local community. The most important ones, however, are taken at the Takhts. These decisions are made after a meeting of the leaders of the Takhts, guided by the Shiromani Gurdwara Parbandhak Committee (SGPC). Guidance about the meaning of passages from the Guru Granth Sahib can also come from the Takhts.

The Five Takhts and where they are to be found are listed in the table below.

Name	Place
Akal Takht	Amritsar
Takht Keshgarh	Anandpur
Takht Hazur	Nanded
Takht Harimandir	Patna
Takht Damdama Sahib	Talwandi Sabo

● AKAL TAKHT

Guru Hargobind laid the foundations of **Akal Takht**, the building that faces the Golden Temple. This is one of the names of God and means 'throne of the Timeless One'.

Inside Akal Takht is a large throne which stands for Sikh rule. Akal Takht probably has the most influence over important decisions. It is the place where most of the important conferences have been held since the death of Guru Gobind Singh.

Outside there are two Nishans Sahib, showing that it is a gurdwara. Worship takes place there every day.

● THE OTHER TAKHTS

The last four Takhts are all connected with Guru Gobind Singh.

The Takht at Anandpur is important because it is connected with the Khalsa. The celebrations of the festivals of Vaisakhi and Hola Mahalla take place there.

The Takht at Nanded stands on the place where Guru Gobind Singh died. The Guru Granth Sahib is read there day and night.

The Takht at Patna is at the place where Guru Gobind Singh was born. Many articles that belonged to the Guru are on display.

The Takht at Talwandi Sabo is where Guru Gobind Singh produced the final version of the Guru Granth Sahib.

◀ *Akal Takht faces Harimandir and has two Nishans Sahib beside it*

Important Gurdwaras

There are other important gurdwaras for Sikhs. These are normally associated with particular Gurus. They are places that Sikhs might visit, given the opportunity. A list of the most important is given opposite.

Name	Place	Guru
Nankana Sahib	near Lahore	Guru Nanak
Darbar Sahib	Tarn Taran	Guru Arjan
(None given)	Kartarpur	Guru Nanak
Baoli Sahib	Goindwal	Guru Amar Das
Sis Ganj	Delhi	Guru Tegh Bahadur

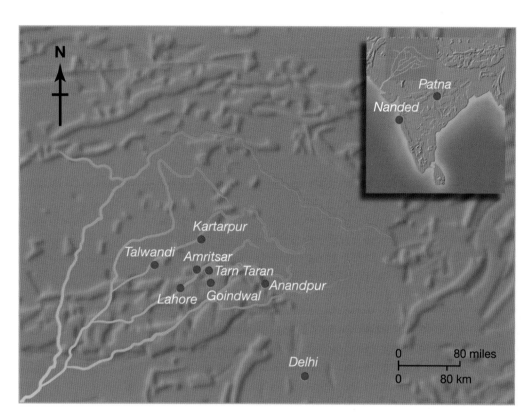

◄ *A map showing where the five Takhts and the important gurdwaras can be found*

1 a) Look at the word search opposite. You will find the names of five important places in India mentioned in this chapter. When you have found them write them down.

b) Next to the places you have found write the name of the Takht or gurdwara that can be found there.

c) Write a sentence about each of the Takhts you have written down.

2 a) Who laid the foundations of Akal Takht?

b) Where could you find Akal Takht?

c) Why is Akal Takht the most important of all the Takhts?

3 Explain the importance of the Takhts in Sikhism.

4 Some decisions can be taken by individuals, others by the local community and others are taken by the Takhts. In groups discuss what sort of decisions might be taken by each group. Note them down, and share your ideas with the rest of the class.

5 What are the important decisions at school? Who should be involved in taking them? Give reasons for your answer.

R	I	H	D	E	L	H	I
U	E	P	L	U	A	D	P
P	S	M	A	I	H	L	A
D	A	H	T	R	O	K	W
N	O	T	A	G	R	A	I
A	N	A	N	D	E	D	L
N	H	U	R	A	L	T	S
A	R	D	H	D	K	I	D

Many larger gurdwaras will have other special rooms. There might be a museum with **relics** from famous Sikhs, and maybe models of the important gurdwaras of the Five Takhts. Also there may be an art gallery. In the gallery there will be pictures of the ten Gurus. There may also be pictures of other famous Sikhs. Many are martyrs who met horrible deaths, but would not give up their faith. They are Sikhs whose devotion to God sets a good example for all other Sikhs.

● Mai Bhago

Mai Bhago was a Sikh woman who lived at the time of Guru Gobind Singh. She was born in a village near Amritsar.

The rulers demanded that the Sikhs leave Anandpur. They said that anyone who did not follow the Guru would be left untouched. Forty Sikhs told Guru Gobind Singh that they were not Sikhs any more. They were told to write down their decision and sign it. Mai Bhago was upset to hear that some Sikhs who had gone to Anandpur to fight for Guru Gobind Singh had then deserted him. She met the deserters and persuaded them to apologise to the Guru. She then went with them to find the Guru.

Guru Gobind Singh had to leave Anandpur. His two youngest sons went with their grandmother. His elder sons lost their lives in a battle. The emperor's forces pursued the Guru. Mai Bhago and the men she was leading fought the emperor's army. They fought so fiercely that the army had to retreat. All forty Sikhs lost their lives in the battle. Mai Bhago was injured in the battle, but survived.

Guru Gobind Singh took care of Mai Bhago. When she recovered she stayed with the Guru as one of his bodyguards. After the Guru died she retired and meditated. She lived to an old age. Her house has been made into a gurdwara. It is named after her. Her faith and bravery are an example to all Sikhs, and show how women can play an equal role to men.

► *Mai Bhago, a brave Sikh woman*

● The Sahibzadas

The Sahibzadas was the name give to the sons of Guru Gobind Singh. The two younger sons, Baba Zorawar Singh and Baba Fateh Singh, had left the fort at Anandpur with their grandmother, Mata Gujri. At one time on their journey they were sheltered in a Muslim home.

They then went on to stay in the home of one of the Guru's servants. While they were there their gold was stolen by the servant. When Mata Gujri asked the servant about the disappearance of the gold, he became angry. He went to Kotwal, the district centre, and told the Director that the Guru's mother and two of his sons were hiding in his house. Constables were sent with the servant to arrest them. The servant received a huge sum of money as a reward.

The Guru's sons were taken to the court of the Nawab (Ruler). Everyone was impressed by their lack of fear and devotion to God. The Nawab asked them to give up their religion. He said they could have anything they wanted. They replied:

> ● We don't care for worldly wealth. Nothing will make us give up our religion.

The ruler was advised to release the boys as they had not committed any crime. He called them rebels because they would not obey his orders, which were unjust. The Sahibzadas told the Nawab that they would go on fighting until his rule was wiped out. A government official heard this and said that they should not be released. They showed no fear.

The order was given that they should be bricked up, alive. Another ruler, whose brother had been killed by Guru Gobind Singh in battle, said that this punishment was a sin, as the children were very young.

◀ *Mata Gujri and the Sahibzadas are arrested*

However, the Nawab arranged for the sentence to be carried out. Two other prisoners were granted freedom for carrying out the terrible deed. The boys were given another chance to give up their Sikh faith. Again they replied:

> ● We shall never give up our faith . . . Death has no meaning for us.

A wall was built around the two boys. As it got higher the Sahibzadas again refused to give up their Sikh beliefs. The boys became unconscious. This upset those building the wall. They decided to pull down the wall. They pulled out the bodies of the unconscious boys, and killed them. Before news of their death could be brought to their grandmother she, too, died.

The younger Sahibzadas are just two of the martyrs who give strength to Sikhs. Their example encourages Sikhs to be courageous and strong when tormented. They were given lots of chances to change their faith. They were not attracted by worldly riches, nor life itself. Nothing could shake their Sikh faith.

A Hindu poet wrote:

> ● . . . the future of a community whose sons can lay down their lives for their faith is bound to be glorious.

▶ *The wall is built around the Sahibzadas who show no fear*

1 **a)** Read the story of Mai Bhago very carefully.
   b) In pairs discuss and decide what you consider to be the *four* most important events in the story. Note them down.
   c) On your own, divide a page into four equal parts. Draw a picture to show each of the events. Write a suitable caption underneath to explain what the picture shows.

2 **a)** Read the story of the Sahibzadas very carefully.

   b) Imagine that you were a newspaper reporter at the time. Write the story of the Sahibzadas in the style of a modern newspaper report, with a headline and a picture.

3 **a)** Write a sentence to explain what a martyr is.
   b) There have been many Sikh martyrs. In groups discuss what personal qualities Mai Bhago and the Sahibzadas showed that make them good examples for Sikhs. Share your findings with the rest of the class.

4 How does having martyrs as examples of faith help religious people?

Maharaja Ranjit Singh

After the death of Guru Gobind Singh in 1708 CE the persecution of Sikhs continued. But the strength of the emperor was fading away. The Sikhs set up military groups called 'misls' to defend the Punjab. It was into the ruling family of one of these misls that Ranjit Singh was born in 1780 CE.

He became leader at the age of twelve in 1792. In 1799 CE he captured the city of Lahore and made it his capital. He united the military groups and soon became Maharaja, which means great king.

He lived in a simple way. He was brave and courageous. He was known as the 'Lion of the Punjab'.

Amritsar became part of his empire in 1802 CE. He visited Harimandir and washed in the tank. A council to govern Harimandir was set up. He did a lot of work on the building including putting on the golden roof. He also provided beautiful marble work, paintings, the hall of mirrors and gold work inside. He built the deori, the silver-covered gate, at the entrance to the walkway across the tank.

During his reign other gurdwaras were repaired and more were set up.

His rule was a time of peace, tolerance and fairness to others, no matter who they were. His army included Muslims, Hindus and Sikhs at all levels. The Akali Sikhs, who later became known as the Nihangs, were in his army. They are well known for their bravery and their willingness to die for their Sikh beliefs.

The ministers of his court included Hindus, Muslims, Britons and Americans as well as Sikhs! Religion, caste or nationality was no barrier in the time of Maharaja Ranjit Singh.

He died in 1839 CE and is remembered for the fairness with which he treated all people. He is an example of the good things that can be achieved by using Sikh beliefs to rule a country.

▲ *Maharaja Ranjit Singh*

1 **a)** Sikhs remember Maharaja Ranjit Singh as a great leader. Why do you think they believe this?

  b) Write down a list of words that you think could be used to describe Maharaja Ranjit Singh.

2 Maharaja Ranjit Singh is remembered for his fairness to all people. In groups discuss how you might improve society so that it treats all people more fairly. Share your ideas with other groups.

3 In pairs design a poster to encourage people to treat everyone more fairly.

● Bhagat Puran Singh

> ● There can be no love of God without active service.
>
> *Japji*

Bhagat Puran Singh was born in 1904, in the Ludhiana district near Lahore. He was born a Hindu, but found inspiration in the teachings of Sikhism.

He loved learning but came from a poor family. Because of this he had little proper education. Instead he turned his attention to helping those in need. He helped out at the Gurdwara Dehra Sahib in Lahore.

At the age of nineteen he vowed never to marry, so that he could devote his energies to helping the needy. For many years he spent his time in Lahore. He made the streets safe by clearing rubble, and made sure that those who died with no family were properly cremated.

In 1934, while helping at the gurdwara, he found a deserted crippled child. For many years he cared for the boy, who was known as Piara Singh. He carried the boy around on his back as he went about his daily business. He was just like a loving parent.

In 1947 Bhagat Puran Singh founded the 'Pingalwara'. This means 'Home for the Handicapped'. It started with just a few tents in which to care for the poor, sick and dying. Today they are cared for in proper buildings.

The Pingalwara is supported by grants from the SGPC and other charities. There are collection boxes to support the Pingalwara in towns and cities across the Punjab. Sikhs throughout the world raise money to support its work.

Bhagat Puran Singh was nominated for the Nobel Peace Prize in 1991. He was known as the 'Mother Teresa of Punjab' and the 'bearded saint of Amritsar'. He died in 1992, but the work of the Pingalwara continues.

The SGPC set up a special award for social service in the name of Bhagat Puran Singh. He was and is a great example of Sikh belief and practice of seva.

Khushwant Singh, the famous Sikh writer, said that he . . .

> ● had nothing except his single-minded dedication to serve the poor and needy. And yet he was able to help thousands of lepers, mentally and physically handicapped and the dying.

◀ *Bhagat Puran Singh spent his life in the service of others*

1 Write a sentence to explain each of the following:
(i) Pingalwara, (ii) seva, and (iii) single-minded devotion.

2 Explain ways in which your life might have been different if you had not been able to attend school after the age of eleven. (Clues: work, leisure, time, money, possessions.)

3 Write a paragraph to show why Bhagat Puran Singh was known as the 'Mother Teresa of Punjab' or the 'bearded saint of Amritsar'

4 In pairs, divide a page into two parts. On one side write down any needs that you think people have. On the other side write down what you would like to do about that need. Discuss what you would need to do to achieve these ideas. Share your ideas with the rest of the class.

Sant Jarnail Singh Bhindranwhale

▲ *Sant Jarnail Singh Bhindranwhale*

Jarnail Singh Bhindranwhale became well known in the Punjab in the late 1970s. He was born in 1947 and became a preacher. He had **orthodox** beliefs and was very strict about his religion. He was known as a holy man and was called 'sant', which means saintly. At the time there was lots of arguing about the rights of Sikhs.

Sant Jarnail Singh Bhindranwhale became very popular at a time when the Sikhs were being persecuted in India. A Hindu newspaper editor who had been strongly criticised by Sant Jarnail Singh Bhindranwhale was killed. It was suspected that he might have been involved and so he was arrested. However, he was released very quickly. This made him even more popular.

The situation for Sikhs in the Punjab was very bad by this time. Even Sikhs who worked with other groups were being attacked and, in some cases, murdered. As the persecution of Sikhs increased, Sant Jarnail Singh Bhindranwhale went to Harimandir for safety.

The Indian army attacked Harimandir Sahib on 1 June 1984, but the Sikhs fought back. The firing finally stopped on 6 June. By this time Akal Takht had been virtually destroyed and Harimandir badly damaged. Nearly 1,200 people were killed in that short time. Among the dead was Sant Jarnail Singh Bhindranwhale. In death he became a hero to the Sikhs. He was an example of the courage and commitment expected of Sikhs in defending their faith and holy places. He is spoken of alongside other Sikhs who have lost their lives defending Harimandir, such as Bhai Gurbax Singh, Baba Deep Singh and Jassa Singh Ahluwalia.

His death and the attack on Harimandir shocked Sikhs all over the world. He was very popular with young people and since that time many young Sikhs have turned to their faith again.

▲ *This picture inside a gurdwara shows the damage done to the Akal Takht in 1984 and how it looks when completely repaired*

1 Write a sentence to explain each of the following:
   (i) misl, (ii) maharaja, (iii) sant.
2 Write a paragraph to explain why Sant Jarnail Singh Bhindranwhale is very important to many Sikhs.
3 Are there any beliefs for which you would be willing to die? In groups discuss this and note them down. Share your thoughts with other groups.

There is no difference between a temple and a mosque,
nor between the prayers of a Hindu or a Muslim
Though differences seem to mark and distinguish, all men are in reality the same.
Gods and demons, celestial beings, men called Muslims and others called Hindus,
such differences are trivial, inconsequential, the outward results of locality and dress.
With eyes the same, the ears and body, all possessing a common form,
all are in fact a single creation, the elements of nature in a uniform blend.
Allah is the same as the Hindu God, Puranas and Qur'an are one and the same.
All are the same, none is separate; a single form, a single creation.

Guru Gobind Singh

▲ *All the sangat sit on the floor to show their equality. Traditionally men and women sit separately*

Jasbinder

Singh

Kaur

▲ *Some of the ways people are treated equally in Sikhism*

The fact that all people are equal is a central belief and practice in Sikhism. There should be no distinction of caste, class, colour, race or gender.

Guru Nanak set up the langar where all visitors were expected to eat together. The Emperor Akbar accepted this when he visited Guru Amar Das. Today everyone is still expected to share a meal in the langar.

Equality can be seen in many of the practices of Sikhism. In the gurdwara all must bow their heads before the Guru Granth Sahib as a sign of respect. Everyone sits at the same level below the scriptures. There are no places of honour. The only different places are for the granthi and the ragis. They sit slightly higher to read from the Guru Granth Sahib and sing the hymns. They do this to serve both God and the **sangat**, not to show that they are more important. Sharing Karah Parshad stresses equality too.

Even the Guru Granth Sahib contains hymns of Hindus and Muslims as well as those of the Gurus. It stresses the contribution of all religious people.

Men and women are treated equally from birth. First names can be the same for boys and girls. The only differences are that boys are called Singh and girls Kaur. It is unity that is important. Members of the Khalsa must all wear the same symbols, called the Panj Kakke, Five Ks. These are signs of a single Sikh identity.

Here are the views of some Sikhs about equality:

- There's only one thing better than any other – that's God. Everybody else is equal. That's what the Gurus said.

- There's no difference between men and women in religion. Any differences are because of the old way of living.

- There are no restrictions in the religious sense on women. Among Sikhs, women have equal rights to men. They can vote to elect representatives, be a priest, perform important ceremonies and do any work or service a man can do.

● The Place of Women

The Gurus did a lot to improve the status of women. Guru Nanak said that:

- It is by woman the condemned one that we are conceived,
  And from her that we are born; it is with her that we are betrothed and married.
  It is woman we befriend, it is she who keeps the race going;
  When one woman dies, we seek another;
  it is with her we become established in society.
  Why should we call her inferior, who gives birth to great men?

This gave women equal status to men within Sikhism. They are able to fulfil any role that a man can. It should be remembered that Guru Nanak said this more than 450 years ago! The Sex Discrimination Act, which gives women equal rights in England, only became law in 1975!

The fair treatment of all women is built into Sikhism. The Rahit Maryada says:

- A Sikh should respect another man's wife as he would his own mother; and another man's daughter as he would his own daughter.

Women are also protected in Sikhism. Child marriage, a common practice at one time, was banned. Also, in the past in the Hindu tradition, a widow used to throw herself on her husband's funeral pyre. This was banned and widows were allowed to remarry.

▲ A woman as the granthi

55

1 a) Carefully read the quotation from Guru Gobind Singh at the beginning of this chapter.

b) In pairs discuss what it tells you about equality. Does it suggest that all people are the same? What does it say about the different religions?

c) Draw a poster to show some of the ideas in the quotation.

2 How do Sikhs show that they believe all people are equal?

3 Read the section on the place of women. What is the attitude of the Sikh religion to women? Use examples from the text and quotations to explain your answer.

4 Do you think it is possible to live in a society where everyone is treated the same? Give your reasons and examples to back up your answer.

5 In pairs design and draw a poster to encourage people to treat women, or people of different races or religions, equally. In your own words explain how the poster will get the message across to people who see it.

The whole of India was shocked. It made Sikhs very angry. They felt that they had to put their demands even more strongly. In 1920 they set up a Central Gurdwara Management Committee to manage all gurdwaras. They were given control of those in the Punjab by Act of Parliament in 1925.

> ● Blessed is the death of martyrs,
> Should they meet death in a worthy cause.
>
> *Guru Nanak*

India was given independence from Britain in 1947. At the same time a separate Muslim country called Pakistan was set up. It was later separated into Pakistan and Bangladesh. Sikhs also wanted a separate state, called Khalistan. They were ignored, and the Punjab was split between Pakistan and India. This made more than two million Sikhs homeless.

▲ *Poster showing Sikh support for the idea of Khalistan*

After 1966 Sikhs did begin to have more of a say in India. However, things went badly wrong again in June 1984. The Indian Army attacked and damaged Akal Takht and Harimandir. Sikhs everywhere were shocked.

> ● I realised I was a Sikh . . . it was me they were doing this to . . . but I wasn't doing anything about my religion. That's why I wear the Five Ks and a turban. It's good to find your real self.

▲ *Special dress helps Sikhs maintain their identity and unity*

Sikhs have always seen themselves as a separate religious group. Events during the twentieth century have encouraged them to stand up for their rights. In the early days of that century Sikhs wanted to manage their own places of worship. They were not allowed to do this at the time. This led to a great deal of tension between Sikhs and those in control.

In 1919 the Sikhs gathered for the celebration of Vaisakhi in Amritsar. As this was taking place the British Army entered the area of Jallianwallah Bagh and opened fire on the gathering. This was not a political meeting, they were not rioters or violent protesters. They were mainly peaceful family groups of parents and children who had come for Vaisakhi. Many hundreds were killed and maimed.

Later in the year, on 31 October, the Indian Prime Minister, Mrs Indira Gandhi was killed by two of her Sikh bodyguards. The whole Sikh community seemed to be made a **scapegoat** for this act. It was followed by violence. Many innocent people were killed. The violence has never really died down since that time.

Sikhism is not just a religion of India. Sikhs are to be found throughout the world, especially in English-speaking countries. There are Sikh communities in Britain, parts of Africa, America and Canada. Nevertheless, their focus remains the Punjab.

The events in India have made Sikhs throughout the world think about their faith. Many more young Sikhs are kesh-dhari and more are joining the Khalsa. They are less interested in the 'bright lights' and rewards that a rich society can offer. They are calling again for a separate Sikh nation called Khalistan.

Sikhs in the north of India are willing to die for this cause. The example set by Sant Jarnail Singh Bhindranwhale and many other martyrs is important for the future.

To many Sikhs they are the ideal saint-soldiers. They showed courage in laying down their lives in the service of others and for their faith. They have set new standards for young Sikhs to follow.

● Let my mind be guided exclusively to ever eagerly sing Your praises,
And when the time comes, I should die, fighting heroically in battle.

Dasam Granth
the favourite prayer of *Guru Gobind Singh*

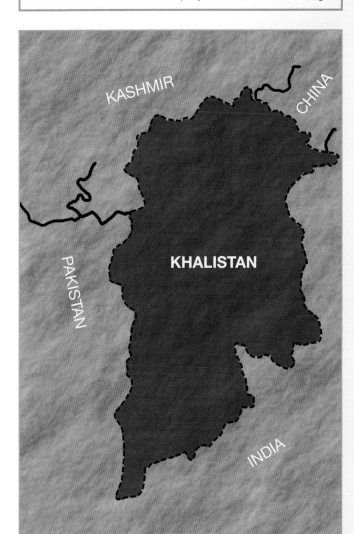

▶ *A map showing where the state of Khalistan might be located*

1 Draw a timeline to show the events that took place in India.
2 **a)** What is Khalistan?
  b) Why do you think it is so important to Sikhs?
3 Imagine that you are a young Sikh, like the one quoted on page 56. Write down in your own words the reasons why you now wear the Five Ks. You may want to refer to other chapters in the book, such as People, What Sikhs Believe, After Guru Nanak and The Khalsa.
4 **a)** In groups discuss why you think many young Sikhs are no longer attracted by the 'bright lights and rewards of a rich society'.
  b) Share your ideas with the class.
  c) Draw a poster which shows some of the reasons you have discussed.

Sikhs are influencing life in India and other parts of the world in all sorts of different ways, especially in the entertainment industry.

● Films

The Indian film industry is based in Mumbai (Bombay). It is known as Bollywood. Most films are in Hindi, the main Indian language, but a few are made for Punjabi audiences.

The stories in Indian films, including those in Punjabi, are often about the relationships, focusing on courtship and marriage. Some recent films have tackled more sensitive issues, such as the life of Guru Gobind Singh. The Guru was not portrayed in the film because it would have offended Sikh beliefs.

A film has also been made about the freedom fighter Shaheed Udham Singh. He was present when the Sikhs were massacred at Jallianwalah Bagh in 1919. In 1940 in London he assassinated the person who had been Governor of the Punjab when the massacre took place. Shaheed Udham Singh was hanged for this crime in the same year. His ashes were returned to India in 1975.

Many of the most famous directors in both Hindi and Punjabi films are from the Punjab. It has been said that without the many Punjabis working in Bollywood very few films would be produced.

● Dancing

The most famous traditional dance known as bhangra was performed by men at the harvest. The performers dress in colourful costumes, usually with head-dresses and waistcoats. They tie bells to their ankles and dance around drummers playing 'dhols'. The drums set the rhythm of the dance. Often the dancers twirl full-length sharpened swords, while other dancers jump over them. They also shout encouragement as the dance speeds up.

These actions may be part of sketches miming the cutting or harvesting of the crop. They are also like those in a battle, so it was good training for soldiers. Sometimes scarves are used in place of swords. The dancing is very energetic and requires great physical fitness.

Though women sometimes join in nowadays, they have a similar dance called giddha.

▶ An exhibition of bhangra dancing by a group of Sikhs

58

● Music

Punjabi pop music is also very important. This, too, is known as bhangra. It has a very strong beat. It uses traditional Indian instruments such as dhol, dholak and tabla (all types of drum) to provide the beat. It was made very popular in the 1960s by groups such as A S Kang and Alaap. Alaap also used modern Western instruments along with the traditional Indian ones. Their lead singer and main songwriter was Channi Singh. Bhangra music became very popular for parties of all sorts, from birthdays to wedding receptions. It is also used in many Indian films of all types. The more modern styles of bhangra use either reggae or rap to give it a different approach.

The first singer using bhangra (combined with reggae) to have a major hit outside India was the Punjabi singer-songwriter Apache Indian.

There are many other popular Asian performers and DJs, such as Bally Sagoo, who come from a Punjabi background.

Malkit Singh and his group are very well known in bhangra music. He was born in the Punjab and was originally with the group Golden Star. He has made many hit records and has toured Canada, USA and India. He has even made a record with Apache Indian for the UK pop music market.

He said in an interview:

> ● I have immense faith in . . . God. It's with His help I've got where I am today. Being a Sikh, I do path (pray) every morning and, especially, before going on stage to do a show. Thus, religion does play an important role in my life.

In Britain there are many Asian pop groups whose members are Sikhs, for example the popular band Safri Boyz from Birmingham. Safri Boyz have toured throughout the world.

Other Sikhs work with different bands, such as Tijinder Singh, the lead singer with Cornershop, who had a UK No. 1 with 'Brimful of Asha'. The name Cornershop comes from the inaccurate stereotype that many people have about the owners of corner shops. Many of their songs challenge such social issues and the problems faced by people from Asian backgrounds in Britain.

▲ *Balwinder Safri, lead singer of the popular Safri Boyz*

1 Write a sentence to explain (i) Bollywood, (ii) bhangra dancing, (iii) bhangra music.
2 Explain why bhangra dancing (i) might be regarded as dangerous, and (ii) might require dancers to be very fit and agile.
3 How do you think praying to God before going on stage might help a singer like Malkit Singh?
4 Write a paragraph to explain the word 'stereotype'. Give some examples to help your explanation.
5 In groups discuss how you think that the members of Cornershop might have felt that made them call their group by that name. Share your ideas with others.

▲ *Malkit Singh*

Conclusion –
Sikh Feelings and Thoughts

This chapter is to help you understand what you have been studying in the rest of the book. It is made up of quotations from the Guru Granth Sahib, the Dasam Granth and from practising Sikhs. All the quotations from the Guru Granth Sahib and the Dasam Granth are in *italics*.

The quotations used state many of the important beliefs and ideas that Sikhs have. They say how Sikhs feel about the world around them, how they have been and are treated, and what they hope for in the future.

● God, the World, People and the Guru Granth Sahib

Holy are the continents created by Thee;
Holy is Thy universe.
Holy are the worlds and all within them.

Guru Nanak

The fool is wrapped up in pleasures, which all result in suffering.
From pleasure comes the sin that people commit.
From pleasure comes the suffering and separation from God,
That destroys people spiritually.

Guru Nanak

By hearing the word
One learns of truth, contentment and is wise.

Guru Nanak

Truth is the remedy for all ills,
and washes away all sins.

Guru Nanak

Worship God and you get all you wish.
Worship others and waste your life.

Guru Amar Das

It is cruel to kill animals by force and call it sanctified food.

Kabir

● Whatever's good and bad in the world – God has created it. We can't hope to understand why. That's just how it is.

● Loving God is what we believe in. If you do, it's easy to care for others and see that everyone is important.

● The Guru Granth Sahib is the centre of all we believe and all we do. When you understand that, you can see why we give it such a special place in the gurdwara.

▲ *Young Sikhs leading worship in the gurdwara*

Worship

The purest of all religions is devotion to God's Name:
And pure actions.
The noblest of all acts
Is the removal of evil thoughts in the holy company.
The noblest of all efforts
Is constant meditation on God's Name.

Guru Arjan

What are the true prayers?
The first is truthfulness; the next is honesty in
everything;
The third is prayer, offered to God for all;
The fourth is a sincere heart; the fifth is to praise God.

Guru Nanak

So do the fallen become approved of in holy company.

Guru Ram Das

- Saying my prayers at the set time helps me. If things go wrong during the day I can see how unimportant they really are. If they go right I can say thank you to God for looking after me.

- It's important to sit in the congregation and listen to the gurbani. Being with good people helps me be good. Listening to the Guru's teachings helps me live my life better.

Festivals and Ceremonies

- We have new clothes at Vaisakhi and we go to the gurdwara. It's the coming of a new year. We go and pray as well when it's the Guru's birthday. We have an Akhand Path in the gurdwara. It goes on for forty-eight hours . . . then we have kirtan and langar.

- The gurpurbs help us to remember the Gurus. They taught us what God expects us to do. They keep our minds on what we should be thinking about.

- When a child is given a name it is very special. They are given Amrit, the same mixture of sugar and water that is used when Sikhs are baptised (initiated). Only the most faithful and strongest are baptised. We hope our babies will be like that.

- Being married is holy. We try to work together and be as one – that is what God wants for us. By living like that we can get closer to God.

Death breaks all family ties, with parents and brothers,
with wife and sons. All must be cut off by death.

Guru Tegh Bahadur

61

▲ *Young Sikhs take an active part in all aspects of modern life*

Personal Qualities and Behaviour

Evil thoughts, hard-heartedness, slander, violence –
These are the real untouchables.

Guru Nanak

Violence, selfishness, greed and anger;
these are the four rivers of fire:
They consume whoever falls in;
Only those having God's grace can swim across.

Guru Nanak

He does not seek the rewards of this world . . .
He does not indulge in loose or selfish talk,
He hoards the wealth of forgiveness,
And burns away his desires by meditating on God.

Guru Nanak

Know all human beings to be stores of Divine Light:
Do not stop and ask about their caste.

Guru Nanak

In order to deserve recognition in the world to come,
It is essential to give service in this world.

Guru Nanak

The true hero is the one who struggles
For the poor and the helpless.

Kabir

Blessed is the life of that person in the world who recites
the Holy Name with his mouth and contemplates war
against evil in his heart.

Guru Gobind Singh

◄ *A Sikh girls sports team.*
Sikhs should play sports but
should do so with regard to
the expectations of their beliefs

1 Read the quotations in this chapter very carefully. You might also want to look at quotations from other parts of the book for extra ideas and information. Write a paragraph entitled *'What Sikhs believe about . . .'* for each section in the chapter: (i) God, the World, People and the Guru Granth Sahib; (ii) Worship; (iii) Festivals and Ceremonies, and (iv) Personal Qualities and Behaviour.

2 Choose either section (i) or (iv) and draw a poster to show the different ideas you have written about.

Glossary

Adi Granth – first collection of the writings of the Gurus, made by Guru Arjan

Akal Takht – 'throne of the Timeless One'; throne of the spiritual authority at Amritsar

Akhand Path – when the Guru Granth Sahib is read non-stop from beginning to end

Amrit – nectar used in initiation; made from sugar and water

amrit-dhari – Sikh who has been baptised with amrit

Amritsanskar – initiation, sometimes called Amrit Pahul

Amritsar – pool of nectar; the main centre of the Sikh faith

Anand Sahib – the prayer of joy written by Guru Amar Das

Ardas – prayer said while standing at the end of diwan

betrothal – a promise to marry, similar to an engagement

bhangra – a popular form of Punjabi dancing

caste – a way of dividing people according to religious duties

couplets – two lines of poetry

Dasam Granth – collection of writings mainly by the tenth Guru, Gobind Singh

devout – very sincere

disciples – followers of a teacher

diwan – worship; consists mainly of kirtan

eternal – goes on for ever; has no beginning or end

granthi – the person who reads from the Guru Granth Sahib

gurbani – (or bani) teachings of the Guru Granth Sahib

gurdwara – gateway to the Guru; the place of worship

Gurmukhi – a simplified form of written Punjabi used for writing the scriptures

guru – religious teacher; 'gu' means darkness; 'ru' means light

Guru – can be used to mean God; also the title given to the ten human Messengers of God, of whom seven revealed the gurbani; finally it can refer to the Guru Granth Sahib

Guru Granth Sahib – the Sikh scriptures, sometimes called the Adi Granth

Gutka – a small collection of hymns often used at home instead of the scriptures

Harimandir – temple of God at Amritsar; also known as Darbar Sahib, the Court of the Lord and the Golden Temple

hukam – a random reading from the Guru Granth Sahib

humility – being humble; not thinking too highly of yourself

initiate – to make people members of a religion or other group, club, etc

Japji – a hymn praising God written by Guru Nanak; used as the morning prayer

Kachha – shorts, worn as an undergarment

Kangha – comb to keep the uncut hair tidy

Kara – steel wristlet

Karah Parshad – holy sweet; made from equal parts of sugar, water, butter and semolina or plain flour

Kaur – princess; the name given to all Sikh females

Kesh – uncut hair

kesh-dhari – Sikh who wears uncut hair

Khalsa – the pure community of initiated Sikhs

Khanda – the symbol of Sikhism, consisting of a double-edged sword, two single-edged swords and a circle; also the name of the double-edged sword

Kirpan – single-edged sword

kirtan – singing the hymns from the Guru Granth Sahib

langar – where free meals were served to visitors

martyr – a person who dies for what he or she believes in

mission – purpose or duty

Mul Mantra – prayer setting out the Sikh idea of God and other central beliefs

Nishan Sahib – the furled flag outside the gurdwara

Nit nem – the daily rule

orthodox – generally accepted

palki – the structure in which the Guru Granth Sahib rests after being ceremonially installed

Panj Kakke – the Five Ks

Panj Pyares – the five beloved ones; the first five initiated members of the Khalsa

pyre – a pile of wood

ragi – musician and singer of the hymns from the Guru Granth Sahib

Rahit Maryada – the code of conduct of the Khalsa; sometimes called *Reht*, *Rehat* or *Rahat Maryada*

Rehiras – evening prayers

relic – an object associated with a faith leader, having meaning for believers

romala – beautifully embroidered cover placed over the Guru Granth Sahib

sangat – the Sikh community or congregation; sometimes called the sat sangat or community of true believers

scapegoat – someone who takes the blame for something they did not do

seva – service; can be intellectual, manual or material

Sikh – from the word 'sishya' meaning 'disciple'

Singh – lion; the name given to all Sikh males

Sohilla – prayers said last thing at night

spiritual – things of a deeply personal or religious nature

symbol – something that stands for something else

takht – throne for the Guru Granth Sahib; a seat of spiritual authority

Vaisakhi/Diwali – days when Sikhs gather together

Waheguru – Wonderful Lord

Index